CW00521856

Wanderings

Finding meaning on a 1001 mile trek through Britain

Debbie Cunningham

Copyright © 2023 Debbie Cunningham

All rights reserved

No part of this book may be reproduced, or stored in a retrieval system, or transmitted in any form or by any means, electronic, mechanical, photocopying, recording, or otherwise, without express written permission of the publisher.

ISBN-13: 9798370519758

Cover design by: Art Painter
Library of Congress Control Number: 2018675309
Printed in the United States of America

I dedicate this book to Terry Inns. You have been my rock, my inspiration and my greatest supporter throughout this whole adventure. Without you, there would be no story to tell. Thank you.

Contents

Debbie's Quest

Chapter 1 The Quest

We were definitely under attack – there was no doubt about it! We heard them before we saw them, faint at first but growing louder. The unmistakeable hum of incoming missiles.

As we turned round to face the sound, a fearful sight revealed itself. Quickly advancing in our direction, a monstrous cloud-like formation of pure evil. They were heading straight for us! Heart pumping, breaths coming in short sharp gasps, muscles tense, adrenaline surging through our veins, we dove for cover as they closed in on us. These cold-hearted, cruel killing machines showed no signs of mercy in their relentless pursuit. They had only one thing on their minds; to drain the very life-blood from us. We knew they would show no mercy and no human weapon could stand against this vast army. We were outnumbered by at least a million to one.

To make matters worse, darkness was closing in, and we faced the harsh reality of spending the night in enemy territory, with only a flimsy tent between us and them. We were doomed. That's when I learned my first important lesson: never underestimate the power of the Scottish midge!

From the relative safety of the sleeping bag, still adrenaline-wired from these recent traumatic events and exhausted from the extremely hasty rush to put up the tent, I muttered grumpily to myself: "What on Earth am I doing here?" I felt the miniature blighters biting my legs inside the sleeping bag – was nowhere safe from them? "Right now, I could instead be snuggled up in my own cosy bed: warm, dry, and comfortably drifting into a deep, refreshing slumber. Not only that, but I'd be entirely safe from these awful bloodsucking predators!"

But instead, here I was, hundreds and hundreds of miles from home: cold, miserable, and as my rumbling tummy helpfully reminded me.....hungry.

Okay, so I may have been a tad dramatic in my description of the 'Midgageddon' incident, but this humble creature did feature quite extensively on the trip, and I wanted to acknowledge that by giving it pride of place at the very start of my re-telling. That 'first important lesson' may have been a bit 'tongue in cheek' but the truth is that along the way, I did in fact learn many important, life-altering lessons, each of which has had a profound influence on my attitudes, behaviour, and entire approach to life ever since.

In short, this journey changed me; I am not the same person now that I was at the start of the trip. In this book, I want to share with you some of the lessons I learned. I invite you to journey with me. Along the way, you will experience exhilarating, mountain top highs and dark, depressing lows, meet some amazing characters, gain a new appreciation of life, and you may even be inspired to undertake a quest of your own.

***

Journeying. The truth is that we are all on a journey of some sort or another. Beginnings and endings, birth, and death. That's the reality of our lives: nothing stays the same; moments are transient; they come and go. Time marches on, somewhat relentlessly. Most of us get unwittingly swept along the river of life, going wherever the current happens to take us.

For me, as for many others, school was followed by college, college was followed by work. Marriage, babies, mortgages.... on and on.... the great hamster wheel of life. We feel so powerless to change things, to step off that wheel (even if deep down we are unhappy with the direction life takes us in). It's a rare occurrence to come across an individual who fights against this process, swimming against the tide, refusing to get swept along, choosing to change direction or even to stop awhile and take time out. Somehow, that's seen by many as odd or even as failure.

In the summer of 2021, at the age of 55, I dared to do such a thing. I undertook a special kind of journey. For me, it was a deliberate attempt to step off the wheel for a while. According to the Oxford English Dictionary, a quest is a "long and arduous search for something". This journey of mine was indeed a 'quest' in the true sense of the word. A quest for what? What hero's treasure did I hope to uncover? This particular 'quest' was intensely personal. It was an attempt to test my mettle, to discover not only who I truly am but to get a glimpse of the meaning of it all: life, with all its ups and downs, connections and losses, celebrations and sorrows, triumphs, and challenges. What did it all mean? What was the point of it all? In short, it was a time to think.

But to start at the beginning, we must rewind the clock by eighteen months. In the first few months of 2020, the world was in turmoil; the COVID-19 pandemic swept relentlessly through our civilised, cosy lives, wreaking havoc in its wake. The tsunami of change was coming, and it was unstoppable. We witnessed country after country announcing lockdowns. For the first time in living memory, everything stopped. Suddenly. And just like that, the world was quiet. It was as if the entire planet held its breath. That relentless tide of busyness that we had all become caught up in came to a shuddering halt and almost overnight, we were gifted the opportunity to stop, to pause and look around us, for many of us, for the first time in our lives. For some this led to fear, isolation, and depression but for me it was cathartic, liberating, refreshing. It was a chance to take stock of where I was and what I really wanted out of life now that my childrearing days were over.

My overly filled diary was suddenly empty. No social commitments, family visits or events to attend; only permitted outside the house once a day for exercise. This strange, dystopian world turned our lives upside down. All the ways that we thought we knew how to live seemed strangely irrelevant now.

Amid this, all the members of my household contracted the dreaded COVID-19 (thanks to a lack of PPE in nursing homes, such as the one in which my husband worked, in the early days of the pandemic). I was ill. In fact, more unwell than I had ever experienced before. It's a terrifying thing to be faced with one's own mortality. It changes you and forces you to re-evaluate what truly is important in your life.

As I reflected during this time, it seemed to me that I had spent all my life striving and struggling, trying to prove myself worthy of a place in this world. Bringing up three wonderful children, home-schooling (before it was fashionable to do so), working hard to make mortgage payments - there never seemed to be quite enough money to go around or enough time to fit everything in. I never seemed to be good enough or to do enough to be able to relax and enjoy life. I never seemed to 'make it'. Life was stressful and rushed.... I spent my days dashing from one commitment to the next, always thinking about what was next and constantly feeling guilty about all the things I hadn't managed to do. I never stopped long enough to consider that there might be a better, more balanced way to live. It was all I knew, there was a strange comfort in never having time to face things head on, to deal with what was going on deep down inside.

I have no doubt that this state of being would have gone on in just the same way for the remainder of my days had it not been for COVID-19. Being so very ill was a wake-up call. It was during this time that I realised I wanted to do something significant in my life. I wanted to live, in the true sense of the word, not just exist but to really experience life in all its fulness. As a Jesus-follower, I've long been intrigued by those words of Jesus that he had come to 'bring life in all its fulness' (John 10:10). Was it possible to live life in this way? Could I find fulfilment? Was it possible to live out some of my dreams? These were just some of the questions I asked myself during those dark days.

I've always been a driven individual with an 'A' type personality. I'm a goal setter and a planner, a dreamer, and a visionary (some might say I've always had my head in the clouds, and they wouldn't be wrong). In that first lockdown, I came across the idea of a 'vision board', which is a pictorial representation of all those things that I hoped for and dreamed of, even if they were completely unrealistic and unachievable. I decided that I would make one for myself. It was a collection of words, pictures and images that represented my dreams. I included specific things I wanted to accomplish along with some of the fanciful, half-formed ideas I had. I also included values that I wanted to strive for.

I've always had a vague idea that I wanted to complete a long hike, devouring books and movies that featured such journeys.

However, the very idea seemed a bit far-fetched for an ordinary person like me. I'm not young or fit or wealthy. I have work and family commitments that would make the practicalities of disappearing and going 'off grid' for two or three months impossible. And yet, I couldn't quite get rid of the notion that maybe one day I might be able to undertake such a challenge. The idea kept mulling around in my mind, insidiously popping up whenever I wasn't distracted with everyday life. So, onto the vision board it went.

Despite having my life, along with everyone else's, turned upside down and making a slow but full recovery from COVID-19, the pandemic wasn't finished with me yet – it gave me one more gift; the opportunity to make my dream of walking from one end of the country to the other a reality. How? Well, I am a teacher of GCSE English and in 2021, the government in England decided that because of the pandemic, the exams would once again not go ahead. Instead, there was to be a system of teacher assessed grades. All evidence was due to be submitted by mid-June. As long as I found teaching cover after this date for my non-exam classes, that would leave me two and a half glorious months to carry out my mission. So, with the blessing of my manager, that was it...I seized the chance to make my dream a reality and decided to go for it.

Once the decision had been made, what was next? Plan, plan, plan. You would not believe the level of planning that a journey of this type requires. Planning routes, planning gear, planning accommodation, planning a physical fitness programme and so on. Fortunately, I do love planning! I spent hour after hour happily pouring over maps, apps, websites, travel blogs, hiking equipment stores etc. Most of my waking and sleeping hours (when I wasn't working) were spent planning this mighty project.

As well as all the research, I enlisted the help of a personal trainer who specialised in fitness preparation for hikers and embarked upon a training schedule tailor made for me and designed to increasing my fitness and endurance. This involved daily strength training sessions, regular aerobic sessions, and many, many miles a week of walking, with one or two extra-long walks at the weekend, gradually increasing the distance, the challenge of the terrain and the pack weight being carried. Towards the end of May, my sixty-eight-year-old husband agreed to accompany me on a multi-day training hike along part of the South-West Coast Path in Dorset, during which we camped and carried all the kit we thought we needed. It was designed as a sort of 'dress rehearsal' for the real thing and it turned out to be a really useful exercise as we very quickly learned some valuable lessons as to what worked well and what didn't. Our navigation was good, our camping equipment fine but carrying enough water was going to be an issue and we found that the rucksacks we were using weren't going to be good enough and needed an upgrade. We both got sun-burned and realised how essential sun protection would be. We also discovered that hiking all day and camping at the end of it is really tiring!

During the months leading up to the walk, I became quite obsessional and probably bored most of my family and friends to death! Despite all this preparedness, as the time drew nearer, I grew increasingly anxious and began questioning whether I was capable of such a massive feat. I was filled with self-doubt. Had I bitten off more than I could chew? Was I completely crazy? What if I couldn't hack it? How would I cope with injury? Another lockdown? Failure?

These questions loomed large, and although it would have been easy to give up at this point I decided that rather than giving myself the perfect excuse to back out, I would look for ways to make myself more accountable. I opted to put my intentions on social media, tell all my friends and acquaintances about my plans and choose a charity to support. There was no going back now. Pulling out would be difficult; people were depending on me. I had made sure there was no way out.

Selecting a charity was hard. There were so many to choose

from. Many smaller charities had suffered economic hardship through the pandemic, unable to rely on fundraisers such as marathons or coffee mornings. I decided to go with my heart – my own mother had sadly passed away from cancer a few years before and from my work with teenagers, I knew of a charity which offered support to teenage cancer sufferers. And so, the decision was made – I would fundraise for the Teenage Cancer Trust. I set up a JustGiving page and registered with the charity.

***

Looking out of the window at 35000 feet, I saw the dreamy white landscape stretching out in all directions; a carpet of soft, billowing cloud cheering me on. It seemed somehow fitting that this magnificent dreamscape heralded my arrival. My back straightened, I held my head high and I felt for the first time a new sensation: confidence instead of uncertainty. I felt almost as if I had found that elusive pot of gold at the very end of the rainbow. I was about to live out my dream! How many of us get the chance to do that? To follow our dreams? I was struck with a sense of overwhelming privilege and an intense feeling of gratitude. As the pilot announced our descent into Inverness, my stomach filled with butterflies and tears pricked my eyes. This was the culmination of many months of hoping, dreaming, planning, and preparing for this trip of a lifetime. This was it. It was really happening.

We spent that night on the first stage of our journey up north in the youth hostel in Inverness, which was warm, welcoming, and friendly. It just happened to be the same night that the England football team played Scotland in the World Cup qualifiers. We wandered through the city, to the accompaniment of bagpipes and flag-strewn, blue and white faced Scotland supporters. I must admit to being quite relieved to hear that the match was a draw – who knows what would have happened to this English rose if Scotland had lost the match?

In the morning we set off on the rail journey from the civilisation and relative comfort of Inverness to the town of Thurso on the northernmost coast of mainland Scotland. The train took ages. Mile after mile of endless empty moorland sped past the train window and I worried whether our plan to wild camp through much of Scotland was a bit misguided – it certainly wouldn't be easy to camp on open moorland and boggy terrain! It also struck me just how far we were travelling from our home in Hampshire on the south coast of England. It was a very long way and took many hours to get there. What had we let ourselves in for? I was struck by the realisation that there was now only one way back home – not by car or train or plane – but on foot!

Once we made it to Thurso, after many hours on the train, we still weren't finished with our travelling.... we still needed to take a bus from Thurso to get to John O Groats. After slowly making its way along bumpy, pothole filled, winding single track roads, the bus eventually came to a stop at the famous settlement at the end of the world (or so it seemed to me!). We had finally arrived at our destination, ready to start our adventure the very next morning.

Rather than the elation I expected to feel at this stage, I just felt a sense of weariness. After dinner, we took a short walk out to the Duncansby Head lighthouse, which is in fact the most northerly point of the British mainland and gazed admiringly at the dramatic coastline with its islands, sea stacks and multitudes of seabird colonies perched precariously on the cliff sides. It was stunning. It became the first location to feature on my mental list of 'places I would like to revisit one day'.

Early the next morning, after taking the compulsory photos with the famous signpost pointing the way to Land's End, we were ready to set off. With joy in our hearts and a spring in our step, we turned right out of the village and began our great adventure.

Chapter 2 – And so it begins...

Day One:

Walking that first day was hard. No, that's an understatement. It wasn't just hard, it was awful. The packs were heavy, making our shoulders ache. The sun, unaccustomed to making an appearance in this part of the world, took full advantage of the unexpected opportunity and blazed down on us relentlessly, making us sweat and sapping our strength. The only relief came in the form of the occasional shower – well, more of a deluge than a shower! This brought its own challenges as we dripped along, soaked to the skin before our steamy forms n dried out to once again face the unbearable heat of the sun. it wasn't long before the initial optimism with which we'd started the day was replaced with negativity.

We felt the need to stop frequently to take off the packs and give our sore shoulders some relief. This was proving to be much harder than I thought it would be and much harder than the training hikes had been. At least then I had known that there was an end in sight – we can all endure many hardships if we know they are only temporary; it made such a big difference knowing that there was a hot meal and a comfy bed waiting for us at the end of a training day. But on that first day of 'proper' walking, I wasn't anticipating such luxuries; instead, I worried about whether we'd be able to find the campsite we'd booked for the first night, knowing that we had only dehydrated cheesy mashed potato and tinned sardines to look forward to (which was to become our standard 'go to' meal throughout the hike).

Our training hikes had been only a few days long at the most but the thought that this daily struggle was going to be my life for at least the next couple of months was intimidating. The miles stretched dauntingly ahead of us. The quiet country roads we had chosen to navigate to avoid the pathless, busy main road, were deserted and seemingly endless, with little relief or shade from the hot sun. No pubs, cafes, or shops to break our trek. No park benches on which to rest for a bit. Nothing but fields and car-less roads for miles and miles. I wondered how anywhere could be quite so empty. It was certainly different from the busy hustle and bustle of life down south.

After a period of self-procrastination and far too many short stops, I gritted my teeth, plugged into an audiobook, and determined to myself that I would just get on with it – plodding through mile after mile of Scottish rural landscape. After all, I told myself, this was my idea of fulfilment and fun, wasn't it? I was living my dream.

***

Cows. That was the first thing I really noticed. We weren't quite alone after all – there were cows and lots of them! As well as the usual black and white ones, some were all black or all white, but there were also short haired brown cows and shaggy highland cattle. I had never given much thought in my life to members of the bovine species. But here I was face to face with so many of them and as I walked alongside the fences separating us, I really started to notice what remarkable creatures they are.

Contrary to common belief, not all cows are the same - each one had distinguishing feature, from colour markings to ear shapes, from levels of fluffiness to horns or a lack thereof. Did you know that every single cow's voice is unique? That calves and mothers can recognise each other's lows? Did you know that slightly different moos mean different things? That cows even have regional accents? They are truly fascinating creatures when you take time to notice them, and time was on my side. I had plenty of it to spare as I walked through the halcyon landscape.

This curiosity which I felt towards the cow population was returned in full measure back to me; the cows seemed fascinated by these strange looking humans and didn't seem to know quite what to make of the fully laden beasts of burden in human form passing by their homes. They peered at us with dewy soft eyes before telling their friends who came over to check us out too. Some of the youngsters were overly eager to meet us, craning their heads through the spaces in the fences, before being reprimanded with a sharp nudge from a more senior member of the group. I was struck by the similarities between us. We share this beautiful planet we call home with many other creatures and in some ways, we are all the same, carrying out our everyday lives; eating, resting, bringing up our young; getting on with the business of living.

As well as that, I was struck by the fact that we were experiencing exactly the same things at exactly the same time here in this wilderness. When we got soaked through by the rain, so did they. When we got too hot from the blazing sun, they did too. Although we were different species, we were all connected in this moment in space and time and as they looked directly into my eyes, I felt that connection.

We spent that first night on a roadside campsite in a place called Murkle, where we quickly set up camp and ate our rehydrated cheesy mash and sardines with relish. Our feet were sore, our backs ached, and once we had eaten, we collapsed gratefully into our tent. But, despite our utter exhaustion, sleep proved strangely elusive that first night. Firstly, there was the light – mid June in the very north of Scotland has extraordinarily long days and very short hours of darkness. Moreover, we were rudely awoken in the middle of the night by the sound of traffic speeding along this remote, most northerly road. We discovered the next morning that this was unusual but that there had been a very good reason for the volume of cars – an orca pod had been spotted in the nearby harbour and word had spread. Everyone from miles around had turned out to witness this rare sight. I was struck by mankind's desire to be close to and connect with the natural world – to experience that sense of awe and wonder. It makes us humble as we realise that, especially up here where mankind was easily outnumbered by fauna of all kinds, we are just a small part of this big old world.

Day Two:

The next day proved better than the first as we largely followed the north coast and were rewarded by stunning scenery as we walked. We had one problem (apart from sore shoulders) and that was that we quickly used up our water supply. Without the trappings of civilisation, it was tricky to work out where to refill the bottles – no water fountains, pubs, cafes or even public toilets up here. Lack of water supplies to refill our bottles proved to be difficult and we had to rely on the kindness of strangers to help us out, knocking on the doors of strangers to ask for our bottles to be refilled. This was quite a novel concept for the self-sufficient, independent, and capable woman that I like to think I am! This experience was indicative of the levels of kindness and generosity we found throughout the entire trip. We found that on the whole, people are lovely and want to help their fellow human beings in whatever ways they can.

That night was our first wild camping night of the trip. Wild camping involves setting up a tent in the wilderness rather than using an official campsite. In Scotland, this is legally permissible, thanks to the Land Reform (Scotland) Act 2003, which permits the public to camp on unenclosed land. We pitched up among the sand dunes just above the beach at a place called Reay. I was absolutely terrified that we were going to be moved on and spent a restless night tossing and turning, expecting to be shouted at by some angry landowner or officer of the law. What was equally disconcerting were the signs on the beach warning of possible radioactive contamination from the nearby decommissioned Dounreay nuclear plant. I fully expected us both to wake up glowing from exposure to radiation! It was a beautiful spot though which did help to calm my nerves. Taking time in the tent that night to check the route for the following day, I looked with some consternation at the closely packed contour lines on the map, indicating hills – tomorrow's walk was going to be challenging for sure!

Day Three:

As dawn broke the following day, I felt entirely different. All my concerns and troubles had melted away in the night. Sleep had been restorative and healing. As I emerged from the tent, everything was crisp, the air was fresh, and it was another beautiful day. I smiled to myself, thankful that I had been given the chance not only to see but to immerse myself in such a beautiful place. That is one of the joys of camping – it gives you a oneness, a connection with the natural world that is otherwise hard to come by. We packed up camp, careful to leave no trace, and set off once again, hugging the north coast and heading west. The day started well with glorious sunshine and incredible views of the coastline with its rocky shores, sandy beaches, and numerous islands stretching into the distance. Above our heads, wheeling and soaring in the bright blue sky with such grace and agility, two ospreys accompanied us as we walked. I smiled to myself. Here we were at last, living the dream. It was a perfect start to the day. However, that sense of euphoria didn't last long.

***

We had originally intended to walk the seven miles to a place called Melvich where we would stop and have a break, refilling our water bottles and having a snack before continuing to the village of Bettyhill, where we would spend the night. Unfortunately, things did not go smoothly. The road was becoming quite hilly and it was hard going lugging ourselves and our packs up those hills; the sun which had welcomed us in such a friendly manner at the start of the day, had turned against us and now blazed down on us with angry malevolence; our shoulders, still sore from the previous day, were starting to ache and to top it all, my husband Allan became unwell before we even reached the first town. He was suddenly overcome with dizziness, he felt nauseous and became very weak. Being of only slight build, he struggled to carry the heavy pack on his back and started staggering around like some sort of drunkard. Realising that he was in trouble and that we were so far from help was a wake-up call. Four miles in the car was no distance at all but four miles on foot was quite a different matter – it would take over an hour to get help. I made him sit down and rest for a bit, sitting on his pack, while my panicked mind worked out what to do.

"Should I call someone for help?" There was no mobile signal so that was off the agenda.

"Think Debbie.... could it be a tummy bug? In which case he just needs to rest and let it take its course ......what about our walking schedule and our accommodations booked on set dates for later in the trip? Oh drat, it's all going horribly wrong and it's only the third day....no, don't panic......in all probability, it's a combination of dehydration and low blood sugar levels. It's a hot day, he only had a small breakfast, and he probably hasn't taken in enough fluid or calories. Right, what do I need to do? ... ... Water, he needs water!"

I hastily found his water bottle which fortunately still had some in (we had intended to re-fill the bottles in Melvich, so they were running low by now) and made him take small sips of the life-giving liquid. We waited there on the side of the road for a while until he felt a bit better, and I took some of the weight from his pack, adding it to my own, already extremely heavy load. Together we slowly advanced stopping now and again, inching our way towards the village of Melvich. Once there, we found the hotel and explained our situation to a member of staff.

They were so lovely and welcomed us into the hotel, even though they were officially closed to members of the public. The hotel lounge was cool, quiet, and shady. It had an elegant, old-fashioned charm about it, with its dark wood and thick drapes. Glasses of water, cups of tea and packets of biscuits were provided and after a little while, Allan felt a whole lot better. I am so grateful to that hotel and the kind staff who work there – another place for my 'must return to' list!

We found a little shop and took the opportunity to buy some

fresh sandwiches, grapes, and drinks (which after a couple of days of eating nothing but dehydrated food, was such a treat). We ate our lunch in a quiet churchyard in a village called Strathy and then continued on our way. These first proper hills were challenging but somehow, we got through them and the views from the tops of each peak were amazing. The day was long and hard going. It was hot and the terrain was hilly (there definitely seemed to be more ups than downs!) but we met some friendly folk along the way who stopped to chat, charged up our phones for us and refilled our water bottles. Many people we met gave us cash for the charity too, which just shows how generous people can be.

The day seemed endless. We walked for miles. About two miles before our stopping point for the day, we noticed a posterboard advertising hot drinks and snacks. But, alas, the little hut was shut. My feet got slower and slower until they stopped altogether. I rested in a bus shelter. I had never before felt such utter exhaustion. I simply couldn't take one more step. I was spent. Marathon runners refer to this phenomenon as 'hitting the wall'. Allan searched the packs for energy bars which he fed me along with encouraging me to drink the rest of the water. After a while, I felt able to finish the day. We finally crawled into Bettyhill, where we found a pub serving hot food before collapsing with gratitude into our tent, which we set up in the dunes by the seashore.

Lying in the tent that night, accompanied by the soft sounds of the wind in the grasses and the waves breaking on the shore, singing us their gentle lullaby, in no time at all, we both fell into a deep sleep.

Nature was all around us. The sights, the sounds, the smells. I think that for the first time in my entire life, I became acutely aware of the this and realised the connection we have with the natural world. But little did I realise just how important this connection to the natural world would become over the next few days as unbeknown to me, we were about to experience a whole new level of nature connectedness as we entered the 'dark side'.

Chapter 3 – The Dark Side

Day Four:

We awoke to glorious sunshine filling the tent with a golden glow and on emerging from the tent, the most beautiful scene greeted us. Catching my breath, I gazed in wonder at the sight of sun kissed waves glistening on the aqua marine sea accompanied by the sound of gentle ripples contentedly lapping the shore like purring kittens. High above, billowing pillows of soft white cloud hovered, seemingly reluctant to move on from this peaceful scene. As I sipped my morning coffee perched upon a boulder in this beautiful sandy bay, surrounded by its rocky cliffs, I felt the gentle breeze caressing my cheeks. "This is it..." I thought blissfully, "this is heaven." At that moment in time, I felt truly alive and fully present. Bettyhill is without a doubt, one of the most scenic places I have ever been to.

With a sigh, we packed up camp and turned inland, away from that glorious coastline. I promised myself that I'd come back some day and spend more time in this healing environment. It would be some time before we would see the sea again. That was quite a strange thought for someone who has lived by the sea for their entire life. I would miss it – I never really appreciated just how much until faced with the prospect of being denied the simple pleasure of spending time by the sea whenever I wanted.

***

Before I started my adventure, a friend of mine spoke of a word that she believed God had given her for me. It was a Bible verse from the book of Jeremiah in the Old Testament, and it read as follows:

"Stand at the crossroads and look; ask for the ancient paths, ask where the good way is and walk in it, and you will find rest for your souls." (Jeremiah 6:16 NIV)

At the time, I wasn't sure what to make of it or how it fitted with my journey but on that particular day I began to get a glimpse of what it might mean.

We left the tarmacked road that ran along the coast and started to head inland across Sutherland on an offroad track known as the 'Strathnaver Trail'. This twenty-mile-long track was beautiful, bare, and silent in a landscape that was wild and empty. We were truly on our own now. No people, no mobile phone signal, no shops, pubs, or houses now for miles and miles. We needed to live off our own supplies and initiative for the next few days. If anything went wrong, no one would come to help us here. It gave me a glimpse of what it must have been like for the astronauts of the Apollo 13 mission as they travelled through the dark side of the moon. The idea of complete self-sufficiency was both frightening and liberating at the same time.

Walking along this trail was akin to walking through history itself. Along the path, were Neolithic and Bronze Age cairns, hut circles, Iron Age brochs, Pictish carved stones and pre-Clearance townships. It was fascinating to read the information boards strategically placed at various points of the trail and I got a real sense of walking in the footsteps of our ancestors. It was intensely moving to walk past numerous silent settlements that had been burned to the ground by the ruthless landowners, eager to clear the land of people to make way for more profitable sheep farming.

I learned of ancient pilgrims such as Saint Maelrubha (642-722) who brought the message of Christianity to this land all the way from his homeland of Ireland. He himself had walked along this very path many hundreds of years before me. The sense of history was tangible.

As I walked, I found myself beginning to actually take pleasure in the journey. Instead of focussing on my various aches and pains, I found comfort in recognising that others long before me, had chosen to walk this very path, even though they too must have experienced similar levels of discomfort and hardship. The moaning and questioning that I'd been riddled with for the past few days had given way to a new sense of purposefulness and determination.

This new attitude of positivity helped the miles to fly by almost timelessly. As I walked, I started to relax and began to gain an increasing awareness of the sensory details around me. The fragrance of wild garlic, the gentle hum of honeybees gathering nectar, the lush green of the new shoots emerging at the side of the track, the refreshing coolness as I passed under the shade of a tree. It was all marvellous and somehow new. It was as if, by focussing on the here and now instead of on the future, a whole new world had been opened to me. It was both beautiful and peaceful. I was intensely grateful and began to realise that by following this 'ancient path' I was indeed finding rest for my soul.

As we neared the end of the day, we met a friendly gamekeeper, who advised us of a good camping spot, a little further along the river in the forest. Taking his advice, we re-joined the road, which in itself was little more than a tarmacked track, wide enough for only one vehicle at a time to pass along. From seemingly out of nowhere, a car appeared and came to a stop alongside us. The couple inside were curious as to what we were doing and why on earth we were there, in this remote, isolated spot, so late in the evening. Having filled them in with the details of our trip, they gifted us some amazing home-made flapjack to enjoy with our meal and offered us accommodation when and if we eventually reached Cornwall. We felt truly blessed and gratefully accepted both.

With renewed strength and in good spirits, we left the road, set off across the field, down to the river and crossed over, using a rickety old rope bridge. It was here that we would find the camping spot, deep in the Naver Forest mentioned by the gamekeeper. That was the moment when 'Midgeageddon' struck, and we experienced first-hand the true power of the Scottish midge. All my newfound wisdom about the benefit of living in the present was instantly forgotten and I sank back into my old pattern of longing for past, more comfortable times interspersed with wishing time would fly and tomorrow would come sooner or better still, that it was all over, and I was safely back in my own bedroom snuggling down for the night.

***

Day Five:

Despite a seemingly endless and uncomfortable night, scratching at numerous bites all over my body, the next morning did eventually arrive; night inevitably gave way to day. This time however, there was no feeling of elation, no sense of new hope nor of a fresh start. Instead, we awoke to the sound of buzzing and saw to our horror, the black outlines of thousands of small creatures silhouetted on the top and the sides of our tent. Great – they were still out there, and they were waiting for us!

We contemplated what to do – should we stay inside the relative safety of the tent, or should we make a run for it? We knew that we couldn't stay in the tent all day – there was no point in that - and besides, we reasoned, it was possible to outrun a midge (they aren't very fast and if you keep moving, they can't keep up with you). After some discussion, we decided we would make a run for it. We made a plan of attack for a speedy departure and decided that we'd sort breakfast out later, once we were clear of the wee beasties. Like some kind of time lapse photography sequence, we sped through the process of packing up camp and raced off back through the forest, across the river and back onto the road in record time. Phew, at last we could breathe again. We were free of them…. for now at least.

Little did I know that this sense of relief was not to last long. This day, which had started so badly was about to get a whole lot worse. Long distance hikers talk about the fact that the fourth and fifth days are the hardest ones both physically and mentally and that certainly proved to be true in our case.

Water. It's something we all take for granted, isn't it? You just turn on the tap and there it is. Except that, in our case, it wasn't that simple. There was no tap in this bleak wilderness for a start. Our water bottles, which had been filled two days previously in Bettyhill, were now empty. We had optimistically brought along with us a water filtration system with which we had intended to gather water from the numerous fast-flowing springs that Scotland is famous for and transform it into water pure enough to drink. What we hadn't reckoned on was the fact that the spring and summer of 2021 had been the driest on record in Scotland. The springs which we had expected to be plentiful and abundant were nowhere to be seen. The land was parched and dry. On top of that, there was nothing here – not a building or a person in sight. Nothing but mile after mile of bleak moorland. This was the infamous 'flow country'. We were hungry, tired from a difficult night, and beginning to get thirsty, which if you are hiking and carrying the weight that we were, presents you with a real problem. As you start to dehydrate, your strength decreases, your mind blurs and once confusion and weakness strike, you are in real trouble. This was not a good situation to find ourselves in. We both knew it.

What do you do when you can do nothing to help yourself and there's no-one around to help you out? Well, I don't know about you, but I did the only thing I could think of to do in this situation. I prayed. "Lord, we need you to help us out here. We have no water. Help us please." I think God must have a sense of humour as literally within a few minutes it began to rain. A lot. This wasn't the gentle drizzle I'd often experienced in the south. No, instead this was heavy, driving rain. Rain was soaking us through to the skin, adding to our woes. Not quite what I'd had in mind as the answer to my prayer! Our situation was just so ridiculous that it struck me as being actually quite funny. Instead of bemoaning my fate, I started to chuckle, which before long gave way to a raucous belly-laugh out loud. For some reason, everything seemed hilarious (I was probably slightly delirious at this point!).

Then, quite out of the blue, our dire need for fresh drinking water was met in a most unexpected way. The same 'trail angels' who had given us the flapjack the day before turned up out of the blue. Here, in the middle of nowhere, the self-same couple from Cornwall that we had met the day before, just happened to be driving on this remote minor road and stopped a few yards ahead of us. They told us that they were acting as the support crew for their own son, who was cycling from Lands' End to John O Groats with his friend. They pushed into our hands bottles of fresh drinking water, jelly babies and bananas, before continuing their journey. What? Breakfast as well as water? Remember that at this point we'd had nothing to eat so far that morning and how on Earth did they know that bananas are Allan's all-time favourite food? This was incredible provision above and beyond what I'd asked for. Sometimes being in a state of total dependency makes you realise just how utterly vulnerable you are and yet, as I was discovering, at times like this faith comes into its own. My somewhat theoretical faith became more real, more immediate out here, without all the trappings of my modern, comfortable and self-sufficient life. I had in my desperation literally thrown myself on God and he had come through just when it was needed.

I was joyful. My soul welled up with praise and I delighted in the sound of rain on my hood and the immense bleakness of the landscape all around. I felt closer to God in this place of emptiness. No clutter or distractions to obscure my view. Just me and God in this place. It was solitary and had a beauty of its own. I began to find myself thinking positive thoughts: at least in the rain, we weren't too hot anymore and we were heading for a hotel just another ten miles up the road in a place called Altnaharra. The prospect of a hot drink and a pub lunch cheered me on as I trudged through the 'dreich' Scottish weather.

***

Excitedly, we approached the hotel at Altnaharra, eager for our lunch. I'd even planned what I would order. A somewhat discouraging signpost, crafted from rowing boat oars stood outside, informing us that it was now a mere seven hundred and eighty-eight miles to Lands' End. Oh well, at least we could rest a while here. By now my stomach was rumbling and I couldn't wait to get out of the rain for a bit. Finding the door locked, I waited on one of the benches outside, glad of the chance to take off my pack while Allan went to knock on the door. Sitting there on my own, I became aware of the stillness of this place. It was so incredibly quiet. A hush came upon me and as I waited there, I became aware of another presence. I felt it before I saw it - a magnificent stag, standing just a few feet away, watching me. Could it be some sort of symbol? I kept perfectly still, mesmerized by this moment in time.

As Allan reappeared round the corner, the spell was broken. I turned back to take one last look at the stag, but it was gone. Had it been real or was it just my mind playing tricks?

Allan was the bearer of bad news – the hotel was shut, there were no staff, the landlord had a broken foot and said he couldn't serve us. With a sigh, we scrabbled around in our backpacks to find some food. Instant soup and pitta bread it would have to be then, eaten on a bench in the rain. Not a very adequate lunch for the nine miles of hiking through the rain ahead of us that afternoon. We were heading for The Crask Inn, an old drovers' inn on the way to Lairg. Having phoned ahead, we knew that at least they would be open for food that evening and that we would be able to camp in their garden overnight.

That nine miles turned out to be the lowest point of the entire trip for me. After a long, hard trudge through miles of exposed moorland, battling against the wind and driving rain, with still another two miles to go, I felt at my lowest ebb. This wasn't just hard – I had expected it to be challenging – instead, it was downright awful! At several points that afternoon, I just wanted to give up, quit and go home.

Eventually, in a state of utter exhaustion, I threw my rucksack down beside a billboard at the entrance to a windfarm, sat down on my pack, and refused to move. Sitting there in the pouring rain, drenched through to the skin, cold, tired, and hungry, I felt at the very end of myself. My poor husband tried in vain to encourage, cajole and motivate me to continue but being the stubborn person I am, I was having none of it.

At that precise moment, a head unexpectedly appeared from the window of a security hut at the entrance to the windfarm, (we hadn't even noticed the small security hut placed there, although that could well have been down to the poor visibility level) and a man's voice called out, "Would you like a cup of tea love?" What on earth? Was I hallucinating? Had I completely lost the plot? But, no, it was real alright. Fantastic! Once again, I put it down to divine provision and gratefully accepted the offer. As the hot liquid slipped down my throat, I felt my spirits pick up. Maybe I could manage the last two miles after all? Suitably refreshed, we positively zipped our way up a long, steep hill with the wind at our backs (unusually coming from a northerly direction and pushing us southwards), helping to drive us up and in what seemed like next to no time, we arrived at the long awaited Crask Inn.

Chapter 4 – Highs and Lows

Bursting through the door, giggling with relief, and drenched through to the skin, we were greeted by wondering stares and questioning eyes. All eyes were on us it seemed, including those of a small dog, curled up on the rug in front of the fire. We must have looked a sight! Taking stock of our surroundings, we quickly composed ourselves, found a table, took off our wet coats, and sat down, leaving our dripping packs in the entrance lobby. Before too long we were tucking into a mouth-watering home cooked meal. It was utterly delicious, and I can honestly say, I have never appreciated a hot meal as much as I did at that moment. Warmed through by the open fire and filled to satiety, we relaxed and began to pay attention to our surroundings.

The Crask Inn is an extraordinary place. It's setting in the middle of nowhere means that it's in the unique position of being able to offer a warm reception to weary travellers off the beaten track.

The proprietors allow folk to camp in the grounds for the price of an evening meal and the inn has rooms available to rent as well. Not only that, but strangely enough, it also serves as a place of worship for the local Scottish Episcopal Church community. To us, it was more than all of this; it was an oasis in the desert.

We found a warm welcome here and got chatting to a group of cyclists travelling end to end for the Guide Dogs for the Blind society. They afforded us celebrity status and were keen to get our autographs and have their photos taken alongside us (they seemed astounded that we were even attempting this trip at our age!). I must admit that having survived the worst that Sutherland could throw at me, I did feel as if I possessed some kind of strange superpower!

The landlord must have taken pity on us as he offered us a free upgrade on our accommodation for the night – instead of camping in the grounds of the pub, he said we could stay in the relative warmth and comfort of the summer house, although we were warned to watch out for the 'mysterious critter' who lived within. We never did find out what kind of critter he meant and saw no evidence of a fellow inhabitant, fortunately.

Day Six:

It was cold that night and we were glad of the extra shelter afforded by the wooden hut. We awoke in the morning to find a layer of white covering the land – it had snowed during the night ... in June! That could only happen in Scotland. I'm so glad we hadn't had to camp outside in our flimsy tent. Also, it meant we could get away without having to pack up camp. The next day was a relatively short day – only eleven miles to walk, so we knew we could take it slowly, enjoy the journey and get to the campsite in Lairg in good time. We might even get a bit of a rest that afternoon.

As we walked through the completely unspoiled, expansive, and brooding landscape of Sutherland, I got a sense of just how tiny we are. The distant mountains, the towering pines, the moorlands stretching out as far as the eye could see....it was all so immense. I felt humbled to realise that this ancient land, so vast and wild had stood here for thousands of years, practically unchanged, and would far outlast my finite lifetime. We as individuals have such a tiny and insignificant part to play in the grand scheme of things. As well as developing a growing awareness of my place in the universe, I also noticed something happening within me; all this space surrounding me was causing my spirit to unfurl like a flower in bud; I was beginning to open up. My awareness of the presence of God was growing. With each step I took, I could feel his presence within, and I could see the touch of his hand on everything around me from the smallest, most intricate detail in each flower and insect to the sweeping grandeur of the landscape. I was developing what I can only describe as a heightened sense of awe and wonder. I marvelled at everything I saw in the natural world. I felt connected to it all and part of something much bigger than me. It was humbling.

Walking alongside the River Tirry towards Lairg was a lovely experience; we even saw road signs warning motorists to watch out for otters crossing. Otters? How exciting! This place was just so alive and filled to the brim with nature – birds of all kinds, mammals, insects, fish and such an amazing variety of plants. It seemed to me that in every direction I turned my head, there was something new to astound and fascinate me. I wondered whether this was the case everywhere, even in my hometown of Fareham or whether I was just more attuned to it all? Perhaps it was there as well, this amazing variety of life, but maybe I'd just never taken the time to notice it. That was the question I asked myself as I walked along.

We had booked into a campsite a few miles north of Lairg on the banks of the river Shin, which boasted on its website of a small camp shop, selling essential provisions. That was great as our supplies were much diminished having wild camped and walked through wilderness for several days without coming across any kind of shop. We would buy whatever they had and make the most of it until we passed through the actual town of Lairg the following day, where we could properly re-supply.

The weather was changeable but not as bad as it had been the day before and we made good time, arriving at the campsite just before 3pm. It was a lovely small family-run campsite, with great facilities and was all very eco-friendly too. Unfortunately, there was no longer any sort of shop at the campsite, and it was too far to walk into the town and back to get some food. Unsure of what we could do, we went ahead and erected the tent before I went off for a quick hot shower – bliss! While I was gone, the manager of the campsite swung by to check everything was OK for us. Having heard about our lack of food situation, he asked Allan what we needed and made a quick call to his wife who was out shopping at that time. He should have known better than to ask Allan - my husband doesn't always think things through properly and this occasion was no exception. An hour or so later, I was surprised by the guy returning to our tent, carrying a loaf of sliced white bread, a bunch of bananas and a packet of butter – not the most practical things to transport when you're hiking! He refused to accept any payment for the shopping and wished us both well for the rest of the trip. So, we had banana sandwiches for dinner that night and for breakfast the next morning! Sadly, we had to chuck away the rest of the butter before setting off on our hike or we'd face the danger of butter coated clothes in our packs when it inevitably melted in the heat of the sun.

Day Seven:

The next day we awoke to a day of glorious sunshine, which was so refreshing after all the rain (and snow). Packing up camp early, we practically skipped the three miles into town, re-supplied and found an amazing little waterside café on the banks of Loch Shin, where we paused and enjoyed feeling like 'normal' tourists for a short while, drinking frothy coffee and eating bacon sandwiches. We both appreciated being back in civilisation again after our extreme wilderness experience over the past few days.

More unexpected pleasure came when we stopped for lunch at the amazing Falls of Shin: a series of picturesque waterfalls cascading through the rocky banks of the river Shin, surrounded by woodland. As I sat there on the grass with the sun beaming down on me, listening to the rushing water of the falls, I once again found myself brimming over with gratitude and pleasure. We were seeing some truly beautiful places on this trip, and it was good to experience them in such a multisensory way rather than our usual method of rushing past in the confines of a car, hardly noticing anything, let alone experiencing first-hand the aromas, textures, sounds and all the small details along the way.

After lunch we continued walking along the river, before crossing over on an old iron footbridge underneath the railway viaduct at Invershin, from which we could see for miles and miles around. I marvelled at this incredible feat of Victorian engineering spanning the valley. After around seventeen miles of walking, we stopped to ask some locals where we could camp for the night. They suggested a great spot beside the river in a place called Bonar Bridge.

It was such a beautiful evening, and we enjoyed the views of the sun setting over the waters of the Dornoch Firth, with the Kyle of Sutherland behind us. Despite our aching feet and tiredness, it was blissful. We felt closer than ever to each other and enjoyed the fact that we were sharing this adventure together. As I reflected on the day, it occurred to me for the first time that we were making really good progress, and everything was becoming a bit easier: we were now covering more miles in an average day; we felt the need for less frequent rest breaks; moreover, we were in less discomfort at the end of each long day hiking. In short, we were becoming fitter. I felt as if my happiness at this point couldn't have been surpassed.

Have you ever stopped to wonder why happiness is such a transient emotion? It seems to depend so much on external factors such as the weather, our physical state, and our circumstances. At this point in the walk, one week in, I was just beginning to learn the importance of appreciating the here and now and starting to realise that true and deep happiness lies in finding contentment and joy, regardless of our temporary circumstances. But I still had a long way to go, and lot left to learn. The next day couldn't have been more different and would test both us and our relationship in more ways than one.

Day Eight:

I could feel my anxiety level rising with every passing minute. 'Why, oh why, did he have to go and leave me alone like this, with no water and no respite from the scorching sun? Where on Earth was he?' By that time, I'd already walked an extra three miles past the town of Alness trying to spot him but there was no sign of Allan anywhere. It was now five O' clock in the afternoon.

Earlier that day, we'd faced some of the steepest hills we'd yet encountered. It was hot. And hard. We had known from the weather forecast the night before that it was going to be the hottest day so far, so we'd decided to set off early in the morning in order to avoid hiking through the hottest part of the day. However, despite our best efforts, circumstances had conspired against us. Having packed up camp in good time, we went to fill our water bottles from the taps in the nearby toilet block but found the public toilets in the riverside park where we were camping overnight firmly shut – a sign offering the apologetic explanation that this was due to COVID-19. That being the case, our only chance to get water for the day meant we had to wait for the tiny village shop to open at eight thirty. This was an hour later than we had intending to start hiking. Knowing that a long, hot, and hilly day was ahead of us, we really had no choice but to wait. Annoying!

Having finally managed to obtain bottled water for the day ahead as soon as the shop opened, we set off up the notorious Struie Hill. Wearing a thirty-pound rucksack, whilst climbing in the full heat of the day was not easy but eventually, we reached the summit. Once there, we were rewarded by spectacular views of the Dornoch Forth and surrounding countryside from our viewpoint at the top, three hundred and thirty-one feet above sea level. After that 'mountain top' experience, the rest of the day was all downhill, both literally and metaphorically. That afternoon was a long, hot, hard slog towards the town of Alness. And then I lost Allan.

Stomping angrily along the roadside, stomach churning, breathing heavily, I grimaced while holding back the tears. I was annoyed at myself for letting him out of my sight and at the same time, furious with him for leaving me alone like this. Admittedly, he was a much faster walker than me, but up until this point, he'd always stopped every so often and waited for me to catch up with him. Not this time though. After a stressful couple of hours of trying to find him, despite numerous attempts to reach him on his phone, I realised with some dismay that I'd lost him. Once this realisation hit, I found myself overcome with emotion. I think that the heat coupled with the fatigue of walking over twenty miles so far that day had finally gotten to me. I felt myself beginning to crack. I tried to regain some composure and not give in to the rising sense of panic that was threatening to overwhelm me at any moment.

To top it all, I couldn't even get a mobile signal here! Our two sons had set up my 'technophobe' husband with a mobile phone of his own for such an occasion as this, but it wasn't any good out here in the depths of the Highlands.

Eventually, after struggling along for quite some time on my own, getting slower and slower with each step, I decided to stop and rest on a dry-stone wall under the cool shade of a tree, while I tried to think about the best thing to do. Just then, I was caught off guard by a ringing sound coming from my mobile phone. Wait, there was a signal now? Hurriedly, I glanced at the screen. It was Allan. Answering the call, I suppressed the urge to scream and shout at him (more out of frustration and relief than anything else). I tried to ascertain exactly where he was.

It turns out that he had decided to stop and ask for water at a house he had passed, then had turned off the main road some way back and was now in the town centre itself. Relieved and angry at the same time, I could control my emotion no longer. I started to cry down the phone. I felt so wretched. Allan, no doubt riddled with guilt and concerned for me, knew that I was probably severely dehydrated by now and he also knew that my greatest need at that time was to find water and to make my way back towards the town. He told me to head back to Alness, go into any shop I passed, explain my situation and ask for help. At that point, in my weakened, desperate state, physically and emotionally drained from the trauma of losing him and walking an extra six miles for nothing, I did what he asked. I tried hitching a lift into the town but car after car swept past without even a cursory glance in my direction. I supposed I must have looked a bit suspect – maybe like some sort of hobo, with all my worldly possessions on my back: a sweaty, bedraggled, dirty and grumpy middle aged woman.

Eventually, after somehow making it back into the town, I went straight into a small kebab shop on the outskirts, explained my situation and practically begged for help. The girl at the counter looked me suspiciously up and down before fetching her manager, who immediately saw I was genuinely in trouble and from then on, he couldn't do enough for me. He generously gave me two bottles of water and a can of ice-cold fizzy drink. He refused to take any payment and allowed me to sit and rest in the cool shop for a while, before I went on my way to finally meet up with Allan at the spot we'd arranged on the phone.

Fortunately, we had pre-booked proper accommodation for that night in a Bed & Breakfast establishment in the town. After hiking some twenty-three miles or so, carrying a heavy backpack, in the extreme heat of a summer's day combined with the emotional trauma of the day's events, I don't think I'd have had the energy to set up camp for the night. Little did I know that I was about to leave behind the hell of that day and enter paradise.

Chapter 5 – Paradise!

With the soft, fragrant bubbles caressing my poor, worn-out body, I submerged myself in the deliciously warm, silky-smooth water. Water jets gently massaged my achy limbs as I lay back, resting my head on the supportive bath pillow behind me, and sipped with pleasure the full-bodied dark red liquid from the elegant, long-stemmed glass. My body began to relax, and I sighed with relief. Ah, finally, I could rest.

Tullochard Guest house had been a spur of the moment booking – we both felt that we needed a bit of TLC after all the camping and got a late availability bargain deal on an online booking platform. It couldn't have worked out better for us. Tucked away down a side street on the outskirts of the town, the guest house was an unassuming building from the outside; nothing much marking it out from all the other guesthouses lining that particular street. But once we entered, we realised that this was no ordinary, run of the mill guesthouse – this one was very special indeed.

It was run by two gentlemen who were quite simply the most amazing hosts. They took the concept of hospitality to an entirely different level: from the moment we stepped over the threshold, they couldn't do enough for us. Taking one look at us, they immediately perceived our weary, broken states. Our dirty clothes were whisked away, only to reappear sometime later freshly laundered, dry and neatly folded. Luxurious bubble-filled jacuzzi baths were run for us, glasses of wine and whisky produced, chocolate and shortbread offered. Truly, we were astounded at their generosity.

Once clean, changed and almost fully revived, we got chatting to the other guests – a family from the East End of London who had travelled all the way up here to scatter the ashes of their dear departed loved one on Struie Hill. We finished the evening off with a delicious Chinese takeaway eaten on fine porcelain plates with silver cutlery, before retiring to bed.

After a comfortable night's sleep, we arose the next morning to find an amazing breakfast spread awaiting us. Chatting to our host, we discovered that the Teenage Cancer Trust held a very special place in his heart as he himself had been helped by them through a difficult time in his own life. On learning that we were walking for this particular charity, he generously donated the full cost of the overnight stay to the charity. It had been a truly special experience staying there and I'm so glad we had that opportunity.

***

Day Nine:

My wonderful dad, who had been stalking us by mobile text message almost daily (except for the time we were passing through the heart of Sutherland, where there was no mobile signal for several days), offered to pay for us to stay in a hotel the following night, which we gratefully accepted. With the prospect of another comfortable night's sleep in mind, we set off joyfully. We knew the day would once again be very hot, but we were blessed with cool, quiet cycle tracks and leafy lanes, filled with birdsong and an abundance of wildflowers. It was intensely beautiful.

After climbing steadily for much of the morning, by lunchtime we were delighted to find ourselves at the most spectacular viewpoint, complete with toilets and a café, overlooking the Cromarty Firth. It was a stunning view – we could see for miles and miles across the surrounding countryside, flanked by the backdrop of mountain grandeur and the sparkling waters of the Firth. What a place to stop and rest awhile!

The afternoon continued to bring its delights: passing through the lovely market town of Dingwall, we enjoyed cool refreshing ice-cream and a little further along, we came to the village of Conon Bridge, situated on the southern bank of the River Conon in Ross-shire. This was a lovely spot for a rest break. We gratefully took off our heavy packs and Allan enjoyed a swim, whilst I paddled. The clear, cool water reviving my tired feet after miles of hiking was just so refreshing.

Today was a long hike – nearly twenty miles and not surprisingly, after about eighteen miles or so, we both began to get tired. So, there we were, heads down, trudging along without paying much attention to our surroundings or to each other for the last few miles, just concentrating on making it as far as the hotel in Beauly.

Walking along the pavement in an almost trance-like state,

putting one foot relentlessly in front of the other, I was hardly conscious of the outside world, so focused was I on my own internal thoughts. I failed to notice that Allan was no longer walking alongside me, until something happened to jerk me back to reality.

A car horn screamed out just as it passed me by. I nearly jumped out of my skin!

"Wow, how rude!" I thought to myself. I looked up, expecting to see Allan's shocked reaction too. But he wasn't there. "Great," I thought, "he's gone ahead and left me behind again!" All those memories of the previous day's fiasco came flooding back. I strained my eyes to look for him ahead of me, but I couldn't see him. Hmm. I supposed that the best thing I could do was just focus on getting to the hotel where I was sure he would be waiting impatiently for me. I quickened my pace, determined to catch him up.

A few seconds later, another car passed by and once again sounded its horn as it passed. What was this? Some kind of rally? Then it happened a third time. By now, with my anxiety already heightened from losing sight of Allan, I was beginning to question myself. "Am I doing something wrong? Are they beeping at me? Am I not supposed to be walking along here?"

Anticipating the approach of yet another car, about to reprimand me for some mysterious misdemeanour, I turned to see what was coming my way. As I did so, I saw something that made me stop dead in my tracks.

There, behind me, some way back, was a sight to behold.

Twenty feet behind me, raising his limbs to the sky and flailing around in some sort of ritualistic dance, a befuddled, beetle-like creature lay helplessly pinned to the pavement. After a few minutes, it registered that this bizarre chimera was not a beetle at all but was in fact a man and that man just so happened to be my husband, I stood momentarily in shock, and briefly considered the possibility of leaving him there as a roadside attraction, before eventually coming to my senses and rushing to his aid.

As I helped him up, the penny dropped. Those car drivers hadn't been telling me off at all – they'd been alerting me to what was going on behind!

Helping him up to his feet again, I realised that he'd cut himself and was bleeding; he was not only hurt but was also a bit shaken by the experience. Weighed down by his incredibly heavy pack, my featherweight husband had become top-heavy, which coupled with extreme fatigue was a dangerous combination. It was almost inevitable that he would stumble at some point and once that happened would find himself unable to keep his balance. He was nearly seventy after all, I reminded myself.

He literally staggered the last mile or so into Beauly, where we quickly checked into the hotel and asked for some help from the first aider. But we were informed that unfortunately the duty first aider was temporarily unavailable, since she was cooking the hotel dinners and it would be some time before they were able to help. Some first aid. In the meantime, they advised poor Allan not to bleed out all over the hotel lobby! Sighing, we left the hotel, bought fish and chips and ate them in the priory grounds nearby, before returning to our room.

An hour or so later, the first aider knocked on our bedroom door but said they couldn't come in because of the risk of COVID-19. They told us to help ourselves to the first aid supplies they'd brought along and dress the wounds ourselves. It seemed a strange response to the situation, but we obliged and dealt with it ourselves, before spending a quiet evening watching tennis.

It felt so strange to be watching TV - almost surreal. I was glad that the following day was to be a much shorter walk of around fourteen miles to the town of Drumnadrochit and that it would be followed by our first proper rest day of the trip. After ten solid days of hiking, I think at this point that we both desperately needed a day off from walking.

Day Ten:

Traffic. I wonder what image that word conjures up for you? Maybe, you picture those endlessly frustrating times spent sitting in a stationary car, caught up in the congestion of rush hour? Or those insufferable hours baking in a hot car, with whining toddlers in the back, slowly inching your way towards the coast in the heat of mid-August?

Well, a word about traffic - it's an entirely different experience being a driver than being a pedestrian. I guess that's obvious, but I never truly understood just how different your perception of cars become when you must share the road with them, rather than travelling inside one. Yes, it can be frustrating and even boring at times sitting inside a vehicle but that is nothing compared to the experience of walking alongside these beasts. They become living things, entirely separate entities from the drivers within. They can be malevolent, violent and ruthless. In my experience as a pedestrian, they are an absolute menace!

Being forced to walk along busy roads with neither footpaths nor grass verges to keep us safe was horrible, especially when faced with numerous bends and blind corners. We had to have our wits about us and pay constant attention to the passing and approaching traffic. All this was exhausting. There was no respite, no 'down time' to relax and recharge. Any lapse in concentration could be deadly. Reminiscent of peregrine falcons, swooping at speed on their prey, the cars sped past getting precariously close to our vulnerable forms, terrifying us as they did so; at times passing within just a few centimetres of us! The whoosh of air and deafening noise as they passed by was a grim reminder of the fact that we were defenceless against such speed and strength. It was frightening.

Our walk from Beauly to Drumnadrochit was along a road

such as this. The day was hot, and the road was filled with
speeding holidaymakers, treating the route as if it was some
kind of speedway track. It was hard going and not a pleasurable
experience at all. Towards lunchtime, we spotted a small church
reached by a dirt track through a field adjacent to the road
and decided that it might make a nice place to stop. If nothing
else, it would be good to get away from the traffic for a short
while. Churchyards are great places when you're hiking as they
are quiet and often have large shady yew trees providing relief
from the heat of the sun and a bench on which to sit. This little
churchyard did not disappoint.

Time seems to slow down in quiet country churchyards. Sitting
on an old wooden bench under the dappled shade of the
tree, I became acutely aware of the hushed rustling of needles
emanating from the green canopy overhead and the gentle
trickle of water flowing in the nearby stream. I relaxed as I
watched the small army of ants scurrying across the yellow and
greeny-grey lichen coating the ancient tombstones. It all gave
me an overwhelming sense of peace and wellbeing and it was
great to be able to get away from the stressful task of walking
along the busy road for a while. We savoured the rest. Capturing
these blissful moments, learning to fully engage my senses,
developing a sense of gratitude for the tiny things. It seemed to
me that this was the essence of the secret of true happiness. It
isn't about striving, achieving, or seeking recognition. It's not
about looking within for answers but about turning our gaze
outwards. It seems to me that we need to lose sight of ourselves
in order to find ourselves. Ironic isn't it?

After lunch it was back to the same busy road for more of the
not-so-fun bowling alley experience, in which it seemed that we
were the bowling pins! Somehow, we made it down to the town
and by late afternoon we were wandering through the strange
'Nessie land' mania that permeates the quiet lochside settlement
of Drumnadrochit. Thinking it might be interesting to see what
all the fuss was about, we decided to take a look at the visitor

centre but it was shut. We turned around and headed for the museum. Also shut. A tourist gift shop to grab a postcard? You've guessed it – shut as well! Hmm.... everything closed on a busy, sunny day in late June - the height of the tourist season - what on Earth was going on?

Just then, we spotted a small pop-up van selling drinks and ice creams tucked away behind the main street. What's more, it had a few cheap plastic chairs and a couple of tables. To us, at that time, this seemed like a mini miracle. We eagerly took off our packs, ordered some chilled drinks and ice-creams and chatted to the local lass running the stall. She uncovered the mystery puzzling us that afternoon – COVID-19 had struck this small community and one by one businesses had been forced to close as their proprietors were infected with the virus.

Afterwards, we made our way to the Backpackers Hostel (which was to be our base for the next two nights) and made ourselves at home. We were relieved to have survived our brush with traffic that day and to know that we had finally reached our first real milestone.... tomorrow was a day off - there would be no need to walk with heavy packs! Yay!

***

Day Eleven:

Wednesday June 30th dawned bright and sunny. It was day eleven of our hike and it was our first rest day of the trip. After those first ten hard days of hiking through wind, rain, snow and heat, up mountains, across moors and over mile upon mile of tarmac, our poor bodies were crying out for a rest. We needed time to heal, recuperate and be ready for the next part of the trip.

We really needed that rest day. What a truly special day it turned out to be.

The day started with a leisurely lay-in. No need to pack up camp. No need to hike fifteen miles or so in the hot sun. No need to carry those burdensome rucksacks. It was a day to savour. After a leisurely start, we wandered into the village, browsed around the touristy gift shops, and found a little café, where we sat, and people-watched whilst drinking foamy cappuccinos out of fancy glass mugs – luxury!

In the afternoon we strolled the mile or so to the picturesque Urquhart Castle. This magnificent medieval fortress, with over a thousand years of history, in its picture postcard setting is well worth seeing at least once in a lifetime. Meandering through the crumbling ruins, whilst enjoying panoramic views of the loch, was pure pleasure. Carefully picking our way down some time-worn stone steps and through an archway, we were delighted to find ourselves emerging on the shoreline of the loch itself.

Loch Ness was absolutely stunning on that particular day, with its backdrop of mountains and forests and the deep blue water shimmering underneath the clear azure sky. Having been informed that the water level in the loch was at an all-time low, I looked in vain for signs of the famous monster, but Nessie was nowhere to be found. Outside the castle walls, the carefully manicured lawns even had re-enactors and a gigantic, full-size trebuchet to entertain, educate and inform the visitors. It was great. We felt like regular tourists.

By the end of that day, we both felt fully restored and not only ready, but also excited to tackle the next part of the adventure. We were about to follow one of Scotland's iconic long distance walking routes linking the North Sea to the Atlantic Ocean, running from Inverness in the east to Fort William in the west - The Great Glen Way.

Chapter 6 – Towards the Setting Sun

Day Twelve:

The Great Glen Way – even the very name conjures up images of grandeur and magnificence. So, it was with some excitement that we joined this famous trail at Drumnadrochit and would be following it all the way through to Fort William on the West Coast. For the next couple of weeks, all of our walking would be completely off road – there would be none of that awful traffic to contend with. That in itself seemed like a cause for celebration!

Anyone looking at a map of Scotland, will see that the country naturally divides diagonally from northeast to southwest, along some of the largest lochs in the land. This divide in fact follows a major natural fault line known as the Great Glen. This fault line runs along the complete lengths of Loch Lochy, Loch Oich, and Loch Ness. In the early part of the nineteenth century, the Scottish engineer Thomas Telford, concerned about the poverty caused by the Highland Clearances mentioned earlier, suggested that a programme of public works, involving the building of roads, bridges, and canals, would be a good way to provide jobs for the former subsistence farmers who had been displaced by the more profitable industry (for the landowners at least) of sheep farming. Thus, the idea for the Caledonian Canal was born: it was in effect a job creation scheme.

It was a great idea. The canal completes the link between the two coasts and is a marvel of engineering, with an impressive twenty-nine locks, four aqueducts and ten bridges. The hiking path of the Great Glen Way largely follows the same route through the forests above Loch Ness, alongside the two smaller lochs of Loch Lochy and Loch Oich, and then follows the Caledonian Canal towpath, thus taking the traveller from one side of Scotland to the other.

The morning that we started this incredible trail dawned clear and bright and having benefitted from our recovery day yesterday, we set off with a spring in our steps. However, after just a few miles, we realised that this trail was not as easy as we had naively thought it would be: there were endless inclines and descents, some pretty steep climbs and lots of gravel underfoot which was hard on the feet. Furthermore, the temperature began to steadily climb until it was positively sweltering. Alongside the heat, the level of humidity increased and the walk became something of a long hard slog.

Despite applying lashings of sun cream and wearing protective sun hats, before long we began to suffer. We were baking hot, sweating profusely and decidedly uncomfortable, lugging our heavy packs uphill through the endless pine forests, which offered nothing in the way of seating, refreshments, or respite from the unbearable conditions. We had to just keep going for mile after mile making do with our existing supplies and occasionally taking a short break by just sitting on our packs. I had expected this walk through the forest to be full of delight, envisioning cool, leafy bowers, entrancing views, and picnic spots. No such luck here. All we saw were acres and acres of coniferous trees along with evidence of commercial timber and logging operations. Many areas were completely decimated by the felling of trees for timber production. To my dismay, it wasn't at all attractive but instead, very industrial and dead looking. Not exactly a haven for wildlife.

It was hard, thirsty work, dragging ourselves and our packs through the strength sapping heat. In my semi-delirious state, I likened our struggle to that of Sisyphus, punished by the god Zeus in Greek mythology. Condemned to roll a boulder up a hill for eternity, he found that every time he neared the top of the hill, the boulder frustratingly rolled back down and he had to start again. So, it seemed to me that whenever we reached one peak, another loomed before us. It was difficult to believe that we were making any progress whatsoever.

The humidity was extreme, and the air was very still, with no breeze to cool us down. These were perfect conditions for that wee beastie – the midge. As we walked, we seemed to attract hordes of hungry midges, all after our blood. They swarmed around us every time we stopped, even for a minute. Suffice to say, we got a fair number of bites that day! Poor Allan was also suffering from a sore toe, which was the result of a burst blister, so his journey was made all the more difficult.

On reaching the top of yet another hill, after some four hours or so of steady walking, we came upon a clearing in the trees and suddenly, there before us lay the magnificence of Loch Ness in all its glory. After the morning we'd had, we were not expecting that. From then on, we were rewarded again and again for all our hard work with one spectacular viewpoint after another, offering breath-taking views of the loch with the mountains beyond. It was awe inspiring and definitely helped spur us on.

Towards the end of the day, exhausted and dehydrated, we

crawled towards the small settlement of Invermoriston, where a warm welcome awaited us at a very pleasant B&B and where a surprise encounter that evening served to further lift our spirits.

***

Later that evening, a knock on the bedroom door alerted us to the fact that the B&B had a special visitor. Tiptoeing quietly to the main guest lounge, with its large picture window, we peered through the glass at the rare sight. There, among the trees at the edge of the garden, illuminated by the lights from the room, we spotted a small perfectly triangular face with beady black eyes, a shiny wet nose, and bat-like ears. With its long, bushy tail and chestnut-brown fur with a distinctive creamy yellow 'bib' on its chin and throat, the pine marten was completely engrossed in the task of gorging itself on the conveniently left hard boiled eggs, oblivious to the presence of the human audience watching the performance. A hush came over every one of us in that room as we gazed together in wonder at one of the rarest of all British mammals. It was so close to us. We all felt privileged to witness the scene and retired to bed with smiles on our faces.

Day Thirteen:

Walking the seven or so miles along the Great Glen Way into Fort Augustus the next morning, where we planned to stop for lunch, should have been fairly straightforward but unfortunately for us there was quite a bit of construction traffic and timber production was in full force. The pathway we were following was diverted and somehow we missed a turning and found ourselves unwittingly plunged onto the deadly A82. With no footpath or grass verges running alongside and a national speed limit, walking along this road proved to be something of a death-trap. Praying hard and carefully picking our way along the side of the carriageway whilst trying to avoid colliding with passing trucks, vans and cars was not a pleasant experience. Somewhat miraculously, after about a mile or so, we found our way back to the official Great Glen Way footpath and followed it safely through the trees before descending into Fort Augustus. We had made it, without being killed!

Fort Augustus is a pretty place, lying at the end of both Loch Ness and the Caledonian Canal. Its location exactly halfway along the Great Glen Way means that it is popular with those travelling by boat, road, bike and those on foot like us. Its idyllic location in one of the most scenic parts of Scotland along with its numerous shops, cafes and tourist attractions offer the visitor everything they could possibly want in a place. However, this also makes it one of the busiest places in the Highlands too.

We found the experience of being jostled around by happy holiday makers enjoying the day a somewhat overwhelming experience. The dazzling colours of shop signs and bright clothing, the noise of traffic, laughing kids and motorboat engines, the sheer range of things to look at or buy....it was all a bit much after our solitary trek through the serene, mostly deserted countryside of the northern Highlands. We hurriedly took refuge in the quiet heritage centre and sat for a while, looking through the picture window at the busy scene outside from the relative safety of the café. After lunch, we wandered around for a bit before re-joining the trail, this time leaving Loch Ness behind for good and following the canal towpath, which we knew would eventually lead us all the way to Fort William.

***

Canals became our friends. Straight. Predictable. Safe. These marvels of engineering are the long-distance hiker's dream. Built in the late eighteenth century, they played a vital role in the Industrial Revolution: transporting goods and services between cities and providing a valuable link for factories, mills, and ports. The United Kingdom was the first country in the world to develop a nationwide canal network. At one time, these 'motorways' of industry were busy, bustling waterways filled with cargo barges, horses, workers and littered with industrial buildings such as warehouses, aqueducts and pumphouses. You can just imagine how it must have been to walk alongside these canals in times of old. There would have been plenty of noise from the constant sounds of engines, chugging up and down, and the shouting between the barge workers. Not only would they have been noisy but also smelly, dirty, polluted, and dangerous places to be in their heyday.

Today they couldn't be more different. Nowadays they offer a haven of tranquillity from modern life. The rise of the railways led to the demise of the canals. Put simply, trains replaced barges in the transportation of goods. Those ugly industrial barges of the past have been replaced with attractively painted pleasure craft such as the canal boats we saw before us. Colourful and intricate designs covered the outsides and cute gingham curtains framed the windows. They were beautiful and interesting to look at as we walked along. Although some people choose to live on them (and who can blame them?), most are hired on a temporary basis by holiday makers keen to get away from it all. A canal boat holiday offers the visitor a chance to slow down, meander peacefully from one place to another and experience solitude and simplicity, both of which are rare commodities in today's society.

After the stressful morning we'd had of dodging the traffic and trying to re-find the original route, it was relaxing to walk along the towpath of the Caledonian Canal. There was no need to think about navigation or tricky terrain. To be able to simply walk along at a leisurely pace and enjoy all that the canal had to offer was lovely. It was fascinating to observe the unique vessels passing by, hand painted with a myriad of colourful patterns, each one personalised or modified in some way making no two boats the same. Shimmering silver ripples moved silently across the inky black water whilst cool leafy trees provided us with ample shade. And as for the wildlife.... well, what can I say? Relatively undisturbed by human activity, the birds, flowers, insects, and other creatures truly came into their own. Here nature and mankind showed that it is possible to co-exist in a harmonious way.

Strolling as far as Kytra lock, we stopped for a while, resting on a conveniently placed bench, and watched with interest as inexperienced holidaymakers grappled with the complexities of operating the lock gates before eventually passing successfully through them. At this point the trail left the canal, passing along the shores of Loch Oich and following a disused railway line before passing through the Clune Forest and eventually re-joining the Caledonian Canal once again. After a brief interlude paddling in Loch Oich, we made our way along the old railway line trail to the hostel, where we were booked to spend the night.

The Great Glen Hostel, an enormous building constructed of a patchwork stone tapestry and bright red paintwork, was all but deserted, except for one other couple staying overnight as part of their walk from end to end in the other direction. Unlike us, they were taking an entire year to walk the route from Lands' End to John O' Groats but they were doing it in sections. It was interesting to compare notes, but I was thankful that we had decided to do it all in one go. I think that once we stopped, we'd find it difficult to motivate ourselves enough to leave the comforts of home and walk the next section, especially if the weather wasn't great. It would be far too easy to give up or put it off.

Day Fourteen:

The following day was gloomy and overcast. We were grateful not to be faced with the scorching sun of the previous day, but it also remained hot, humid, and muggy – not a great day for hiking. Fortunately, we didn't plan to walk quite as far that day. After a somewhat midgy but rather special walk through the Clunes Forest, with its many waterfalls and where the entire forest floor is coated in thick green moss, giving it an appearance reminiscent of some kind of mysterious and magical fairy grotto, the path emerged from the forest to follow the banks of Loch Lochy. At this point along the route, there was a series of interesting information boards telling of the Commando training that had taken place here, involving amphibious assaults. We also passed the remains of a concrete fake landing craft. The day passed quickly and before we knew it, we had arrived at our intended stopping point for the day.

Gairlochy is a significant point on the Caledonian Canal as it has two locks and a swingbridge, manned by a lock keeper. It was a great place to set up camp for the night: flat, sheltered and overlooked by the Grampian Mountains and the towering peak of Ben Nevis. Having spoken to the lock keeper, we pitched up near the top lock and then enjoyed watching the boats passing to and fro for a while. Before long, the sky grew increasingly darker, and the heavens finally released their pent-up fury as an absolute deluge pelted down. Scottish rain is something else! There is something entirely satisfying about sheltering in a snug, dry tent and listening to the rain hammering down outside.

***

Day Fifteen:

The next morning dawned clear and bright. The humidity had dropped because of yesterday's rain and had paved the way for a much fresher day. Gone was that muted hazy hue that only the day before seemed to coat everything, replaced instead with a clear pure light that served to highlight the vibrancy of the colours of everything around us. Fresh emerald blades of grass seemed to burst through the moss-covered banks of the towpath, complimenting the dark olive leaves of the holly bushes, which crowded beneath the leafy canopy of the beautiful beech trees lining the route. All this greenery contrasted sharply with the azure blue sky above us, the whole scene further enhanced by the reflections mirrored back at us, broken only by sparkling silver flashes of light twinkling like stars on the surface of the canal. It was peaceful and joyous.

For a while, we enjoyed our solitary stroll, savouring the natural wonders of the world around us.

After a couple of hours of walking, we began to encounter people. First the odd one or two but gradually more and more people, all engaged in various pleasurable activities: dog walkers, cyclists, runners. I stopped to chat to a guy who was himself walking the entire length of the country for charity. He had nearly finished his walk by the time I met him. We exchanged details and vowed to follow each other's progress.

Reaching the small settlement of Banavie, we were delighted to discover an enchanting canalside café. Civilisation! It was a truly joyous experience drinking frothy cappuccinos, sitting at a table overlooking the canal, with all its comings and goings. Bliss.

After that, our time hiking seemed to fly by as there was now so much to see on the way. We passed alongside the amazing Neptune's Staircase: a dramatic series of eight locks, lifting and lowering boats twenty metres in just fifty-five metres of canal length. It was fascinating to see the boats travelling through this incredible waterway system. Apparently, it takes an average time of an hour and a half to navigate a boat through the entire lock system here.

Shortly afterwards, we reached the village of Corpach, where a quaint little lighthouse alerted us to the fact that we had finally been reunited with our old friend – the sea. We had done it...we had walked right across Scotland from East to West, from the furthermost north-eastern tip on the North Sea to the Atlantic Ocean stretching out before us now.

After stopping briefly at the ruins of Inverlochy Castle on the outskirts of the city, we made our way into the centre of Fort William, where we had our photos taken at the end of the Great Glen Way by a friendly local. We found the delightful guest house 'Guisachan' where our second rest day awaited us. Knowing that Allan had intended to walk with me through Scotland, I had allowed for one rest day a week from the start until we reached the border of England. The proprietors Carmen and Phil Beale, who we vaguely knew from the past, made it their mission to put us fully back together again and ensure we were ready for next part of our adventure – the famous West Highland Way.

***

Day Sixteen:

Loch Linnhe was brooding and moody but intensely atmospheric. An almost eerie silence enveloped us as we sat in the boat, peering expectantly through the drizzly gloom at the rocks beyond. Nothing. The water was still and seemingly lifeless until.... there.... a slight movement in the water, and all at once a sleek, dark head emerged. A seal! As the boat crept slowly forward turning the corner to view the other side of the miniature island, we saw them. Not one, not two but three tiny seal pups sheltering on the rocky surface, their mother never far from view. Overwatched by the mist enshrouded sentinel of Ben Nevis, we observed from a distance, not daring to get too close for fear of disturbing the natural balance here. What a special way to spend a day off!

Having re-supplied our diminished stocks, re-fuelled our bodies from the delicious fare on offer at the guesthouse and repaired our sore and swollen feet (not to mention Allan's infected burst blister!), I can honestly say that by the end of that second rest day, we both felt fully recharged and ready to face the challenge of the most famous long-distance path in Scotland – the legendary West Highland Way.

Chapter 7 – In the Footsteps of Giants

Looking with some consternation at the massive boulder in front of me, I stood rooted to the spot. It was at least twice my height with no footholds or jagged edges to grab hold of and hoist myself up. There was no way on Earth I'd ever be able to surmount such an obstacle on my own. In vain, I looked around and tried to figure out what to do. Any branches to hang onto? No. Could my trusty walking poles help me out here? Even they proved no match for such a barrier. Eventually, it dawned on me that there was no other option - I'd have to swallow my pride once again and ask for help. I was slowly un-learning the self-sufficiency I'd come to rely on and learning instead to be dependent on others. I was learning the all- important lesson that sometimes weakness is actually a strength, and that co-dependency can be better at times than independence.

Clambering over boulders, was not part of my plan. I never envisaged having to participate in rock climbing as part of my walk from one end of the country to the other. But here I was, in this unimaginable situation on the banks of Loch Lomond, deep in the Highlands of Scotland. Sitting on a picnic bench outside the famous Inversnaid Hotel (frequented in its time by Wordsworth, Sir Walter Scott and even Queen Victoria herself), looking at the stunning view whilst eating our sandwiches, accompanied by the orchestral symphony of the nearby waterfall, I chuckled at myself. Why had I been so terrified of this stage of the walk? The very worst that had happened to me was that I'd been shoved up onto the boulder by the bum in a most undignified manner - what an idiot I'd been!

The iconic West Highland Way is without a doubt one of the most challenging walking routes in Britain. Stretching ninety-six miles, through some of the most spectacular and varied scenery that Scotland has to offer, encompassing mountains, loch sides, moorland, and forested country parks, it's no wonder that it is so popular with hikers. Some eighty-five thousand people attempt the route every year, but of those who start, only about a third complete the entire route, walking from Milngavie in the south to Fort William in the north. We walked the route in reverse, travelling south, which meant starting with the most demanding terrain in the north and progressing to the gentler stages further south. However, fortunately for us, by this stage of the walk we were pretty fit and well able to cope with the challenges that the West Highland Way would throw at us. We also had the added bonus of meeting everyone walking the opposite way to us. After weeks of very limited human company except for each other, it was refreshing to be able to chat to such a wide variety of interesting people.

***

Day Seventeen:

Starting from the guest house in Fort William, we headed south along the road before turning off to face a stiff climb through the forest at Glen Nevis. We then joined General Wade's old military road, constructed in the eighteenth century, which we followed on and off for most of the way. The scenery here was absolutely stunning. We were at the top of the world – both physically and metaphorically. Magnificent mountains were all around us. They seemed to watch over us with benevolence. Our protectors. They were part of us as we were part of them. I was struck by the fact that we were just insignificant specks travelling through this vast country. The sheer scale of them was immense and humbling. The weather was kind – sunny but not as uncomfortably hot as it had previously been. And given the fact that we'd had the foresight to pay for luggage transfer for this leg of our trip, we positively revelled in the experience of walking without the burden of carrying those monstrous packs. All in all, I'd say it was pretty perfect!

But as Newton discovered, what goes up must come down. We had climbed for much of the day but the Blackwater Hostel, where we were booked for the night was some three hundred metres below us. Even though we weren't carrying our usual heavy loads, after our fifteen-mile walk that day we were tired, and we needed all our wits about us to focus enough to safely navigate the uneven ground scattered with granite and quartz boulders on the steep descent into the village. It was challenging but somehow, we made it down safely. Passing a pub, we stopped for a drink before collecting our luggage and checking into the hostel.

That evening, the fear factor took over. Reading through the guidebooks and looking at tomorrow's route, as was my habit by now, I discovered that the next day we would have to face one of the most difficult parts of the route – the infamous 'Devil's Staircase'. The guidebooks and a quick internet search informed me that the route is considered 'difficult' even by experienced hill walkers. Gulp. Panic surged through me. What were we thinking? We are relatively old with sedentary lifestyles. Most of the other people at the hostel were much younger and fitter than us – students mostly. Had we bitten off more than we could chew? Were we about to fail spectacularly?

Deciding that I needed to get out of the room and distract myself with the company of others, I found my way to the well-equipped kitchen where I could prepare our gourmet style meal for the night – yes, you've guessed it – cheesy instant mashed potato and sardines! In the dining room, I was pleased to see a group of similarly middle-aged women. "Great," I thought, "kindred spirits" (or should I say fellow sufferers?). We got chatting and I discovered that they were taking the traditional path of south to north. They'd almost finished and only had one final day of walking left before a well-earned rest in Fort William. Although inside I was bursting to know, I asked as casually as I could how they had found the Devil's Staircase on their walk that day. I wished I hadn't asked. They told me tales of woe far worse than I could have imagined. They almost hadn't made it. What's more they said that there were even more challenging parts of the West Highland Way further down. The part around the shores of Loch Lomond, according to these lovely ladies, was not only dangerous but downright deadly. They told me the route was not well maintained and as a result not one, but two separate walkers had both fallen from the path and found themselves in the loch with its unpredictable currents. I was terrified!

Part of my terror was due to the memory of a traumatic event I'd experienced the previous summer when I'd fallen catastrophically down an extremely steep wooded slope in

France whilst' visiting my daughter who lives there. I'd lost consciousness for a short while, suffered concussion, and ended up with a shattered wrist. I then faced surgery in a French hospital, where with the use of plates and pins, they'd pieced me back together again. Although by this time, almost a full year later, I had fully recovered physically, the mental trauma remained to haunt me from time to time. I was nervous of descents, particularly on uneven ground. Because of this, I'd taken to using a pair of walking poles for reassurance as much as anything else (although my extensive research before the trip had reliably informed me that the use of walking poles when hiking significantly reduces the chance of injury – placing up to one third less pressure on the knee joint). But even with these poles, after hearing the dire words of warning uttered by the ladies I'd met, I was truly frightened. Returning to the room, I used social media to ask all those I knew to pray for our safety over the next few days. I didn't know if we'd even make it to the end of the West Highland Way, let alone make it all the way to Land's End. Anticipating the worst and trying ineffectively to push those thoughts aside, I spent a restless night tossing and turning until the morning finally dawned.

***

Day Eighteen:

The day started with a tough uphill climb past the pipes of the hydro-electric power scheme. I was getting used to these early morning 'warm-ups' by now but phew, it was still tough! Just when I thought my body couldn't take any more of the steep climbing, I reached the top, the ground levelled out and I found myself walking along a particularly lovely path through the heather covered hills. It was glorious – spacious and open with mountains all around us and not a single soul to be seen. Finding ourselves alone in this landscape was cathartic. It was somehow elemental, this close proximity to the wild, untamed landscape. I was in heaven! "Heaven truly is a place on Earth." I mused.

And just when I thought I might burst with happiness, I saw something that made me stop dead in my tracks.

A sign that struck fear into my heart – a small, insignificant looking wooden way marker that read, 'This way to the Devil's Staircase'. This was it.... the moment I'd been dreading. I felt my muscles tense, my heartrate increase, and my palms grow sweaty as I gripped ever more tightly the walking poles in my grasp. With trepidation, I cautiously advanced towards the rocky summit, where I came across a lone photographer taking photos of the dramatic landscape. As I rounded a corner, the boulder gave way and I saw what it was that he found so captivating...

"Wow...what a view!"

The imposing dapple-grey mountains reared into the sky, their craggy granite peaks towering over me, a mosaic of colour ranging from slate-blue to silvery-white. I gazed up at them with an overwhelming sense of awe and vulnerability. These were mysterious and timeless beings, safe keepers of this land since the great glacial movements of ancient times had formed the imposing peaks and troughs I was now looking at.

The sparse foliage clutched desperately at the flanks of these great beings, whilst above me the sky piercing apex of each mountain peak was drenched in brilliant light. A sense of hush came over me. I felt so very insignificant and at the same time, incredibly thankful to be here witnessing this. These were truly incredible views looking down towards Glencoe, enhanced further by the stunning weather that day. It's no wonder that this particular view has featured in movies such as Rob Roy and

Skyfall.

Reluctantly, I pulled my gaze away from the stunning scenery and looking down, saw the path we were to follow. The dreaded 'Devil's Staircase'. Yes, it was steep but there was a well-defined rocky track that zigzagged down the mountainside. It didn't seem that bad at all. Relief surged through me – was this what all the fuss was about? As I relaxed, I started to enjoy myself.

In contrast to our rather solitary trek earlier in the day, this part of the route was quite busy. Everyone we passed was pleased to be given the opportunity to stop their steep ascent midway and chat to us. It gave them a chance to catch their breath. We met groups of students, couples, and families, including one family with a small dog, all climbing up the Devil's Staircase.

One group of ladies were particularly interested in hearing all about our adventures, so we spent some time talking to them. We later found out that the small dog we had seen that day had somehow become lost and that these particular ladies had found the dog. On being offered a monetary reward by the grateful pet owners, they had generously decided to donate the full reward to the Teenage Cancer Trust as they said they'd been so inspired by our story!

I discovered later that the Devil's Staircase got its name, not because of the difficulty of the walk but because the soldiers who were part of General Wade's road building programme were very unsteady on their feet after a night of drinking in the Kingshouse Hotel and on cold winter's nights, some of them didn't make it back up the steep path to the Blackwater Dam where they were based; it was rumoured that the devil had claimed his own!

In the early afternoon, having descended the steep hill and joined the path running between the River Etive and the A82, on our way to the Kingshouse Bunkhouse, a minor catastrophe happened. Allan, who was walking just ahead of me at this point, suddenly lost his footing and once again fell. More grazed hands and small cuts on his face but nothing too serious thank goodness. Fortunately, we didn't have much further to go so he limped his way to the Bunkhouse where we spent the rest of the afternoon just chilling in the late afternoon sun and smugly enjoyed seeing all the youngsters hobbling towards the bunkhouse. Our feet were fine on this part of the walk, due in no small part to the baggage transfer service we'd paid for.

In the bunkhouse, we met an interesting chap by the name of Richard and got chatting. We were interested to learn about some of the other long-distance walks he'd completed such as the Camino Way in Spain (quite inspiring – maybe our next adventure?).

Day Nineteen:

The following morning, we were sad to discover that Richard, the guy we'd met the previous day, was poorly - he had an upset tummy and was worried he wouldn't be able to complete the trail. Fortunately, I had brought ample supplies of appropriate medication for just such a time. Having supplied him with drugs, we wished him all the best, said goodbye and set off.

Little did we realise at the time that this was not the last time on our trip that we would see Richard.

⁎

Bleak, desolate and wonderful – that's how I'd describe the fifty square miles that make up Rannoch Moor. Walking through this vast area of emptiness on an overcast and somewhat moody day is an experience I will forever treasure in my heart.

Notoriously depressing - wet and filled with 'lochans' (miniature lochs) formed from the boggy, heather covered land - it has a reputation for being not only 'dreich' but also in some parts quite dangerous. An unprepared walker has a fairly good chance before long of finding themselves knee deep in brown, murky water.

However, at the time we crossed over the moor, it was experiencing something of a draught: dry, firm underfoot and carpeted by an amazing array of wildflowers, among them resplendent purple foxgloves; delicate daisies and buttercups, with their pop of bright yellow; pink fluffy scabia; yellow hawkweed; and many splendid wild orchids. With clear views of the Campsie Hills before us and wonderful Glencoe with its majestic heights behind us, we made our way through this infamously moody landscape savouring every minute.

Eventually the path through the moorland gave way to gently wooded slopes, passing beside the Inveroran Hotel, before a steep ascent. At this point the route descends all the way down into the infamously midge-infested Bridge of Orchy. We found the guidebooks do not lie and hurriedly taking refuge in the Bridge of Orchy Inn, we enjoyed a midge-free pub lunch. I'd had my fair share of the horrors of Scottish midges and wasn't keen to repeat the experience. Although, as I soon found out, they weren't quite ready to part company with me just yet.

There were nineteen miles to walk that day and although we enjoyed the walk, we were grateful to finally arrive at the campsite in Tyndrum, where we had booked a wooden camping pod for the night, thinking that this would save us from the plague of midges we expected to find here.

Well, if we thought the Bridge of Orchy was 'midgy' when we passed through, Tyndrum was on another level entirely! There were great clouds of them everywhere in the campsite. They were an absolute nightmare. Cooking an evening meal proved challenging as did making a cup of tea. They'd even found their way into the enclosed kitchen facilities. In the end, we gave up and made do with just some instant soup sachets and pitta bread left over from our supplies. However, dead midges floating on the top of my instant soup is not an experience I'd like to repeat!

Giving up on dinner and beating a hasty retreat to the camping pod, we had expected to find it a safe haven from them but sadly that was not the case. The very pod itself contained hundreds of the wee beasties lining the walls and lurking on the inside of the small window. Whenever we opened the window or the door to let them out, hundreds more came inside! It was horrible. Ugh....

To say this was one of the low points of the trip would be an understatement.

That evening, tired, fed up with the constant battle to avoid those horrible midges and severely calorie deficient, we found ourselves taking out our misery on each other. We were both well and truly fed up. The West Highland Way was proving to be something of a rollercoaster. No wonder that so many people give up before completing the trail.

When my dad texted his daily message of encouragement, and asked where I'd be on the following Sunday, I found myself replying negatively in a somewhat melodramatic tone, "Some midge-infested campsite in the middle of nowhere, being eaten alive no doubt. But that's only if I actually survive walking past Loch Lomond!"

Day Twenty:

Still feeling the effects of the previous night, we set off along the West Highland Way trail again the following day, which led us through the beautiful and fragrant Caledonian Pine Forest.

There were lots of ups and downs along the way and still plenty of midges to contend with. It was extremely tiring but very lovely and we enjoyed the walk that morning.

After stopping briefly in the village of Crianlarich for a spot of lunch, which consisted only of a few houses and a village store (fortunately selling sandwiches), we ascended to more open landscape where we walked along a ridge and enjoyed some great views before passing under the lowest underpass it's possible to go through. Doing so, with a fully laden backpack would have been interesting, but fortunately we only had day packs to carry.

Emerging from the tunnel which passed beneath the busy A82, we were surprised and delighted to bump into a family we'd met on the Great Glen Way a couple of weeks back. The couple were travelling with their two children and a dog called Nessie. A dog who it turns out, had his very own Instagram account where he posted regular updates about his adventures in the Scottish Highlands. He had quite a following!

Feeling cheered by this 'chance' encounter, we sped towards the campsite of Beinglas, where we were to spend the night. This part of the trail was lovely: numerous waterfalls, many of them hidden from plain sight, pretty views of the surrounding countryside, and rich, varied woodland.

Beinglas campsite was an oasis on the trail. It was a well-equipped campsite, in a beautiful location and even had a bar serving hot food! Bliss. What's more, there were very few midges here. Having eaten a delicious and satisfying cooked meal that evening, I began to relax and tried not to think about tomorrow's hike, when we'd have to face the much rumoured horrors of the Loch Lomond section of the West Highland Way.

***

Day Twenty-One:

Swooshing through dew coated ferns, many of which were much higher than head height, and picking my way over sodden grassy paths, trying to avoid the very wettest or muddiest parts, I felt like an Amazonian explorer, trekking fearlessly through the virgin rainforest, daring to go where no man had gone before. The day was fresh and bright and so far, no major challenges had presented themselves. This wasn't too bad at all so far. After a couple of miles, the jungle relinquished its grip on the land and Loch Lomond suddenly appeared as if by magic as we crested a ridge.

There it was. I caught my breath. The teardrop shaped loch spread out before us underneath the Tuscan blue sky, its waters shimmering like quicksilver, its shores flanked by verdant forests, nestling securely among The Trossachs. From our lofty viewpoint, we were giants looking into the mirror of the world.

From that point on, the trail became increasingly more difficult – lots of ups and downs and very uneven ground with tree roots and loose rocks underfoot. We found ourselves carefully picking our way along, watching our step and trying to avoid the many tripping hazards along the route. We made slow but steady progress until faced with the unsurmountable boulder described at the start of the chapter.

Somehow, we got through the day and although I didn't find the trail beside Loch Lomond as dangerous as I'd feared it would be, it was still a very challenging and tiring day, especially for Allan as unfortunately he managed to twist his ankle a couple of miles before the end and had to limp the rest of the way. It was a relief to finally arrive at the idyllically placed lochside Rowardennan Hostel where we were to spend the night.

***

Day Twenty-Two:

From that point on, the trail became much easier – we were now entering the final stages of the route and found ourselves walking on flat, level paths for much of the way. Loch Lomond divides the Highlands from the Lowlands of Scotland, and consequently the landscape experiences a dramatic change at this point. The lofty mountain grandeur of the Highlands gives way to the gentle rolling hills of the borders.

After leaving the hostel at Rowardennan, we followed the path through woodland and alongside a road before arriving at the village of Balmaha, home of the famous Scottish walker and broadcaster Tom Weir. We had lunch here and spent some time looking around the Trossachs National Park Centre, learning about the flora and fauna of the area. This includes red squirrels, buzzards and hen harriers. I was interested to discover that one of the twenty islands in the loch was even home to a pair of Golden Eagles.

The afternoon brought us great views of the islands in the loch but also a few drenchings from some particularly heavy downpours. We arrived in Drymen about 4pm, stopping for tea and cake in the village before heading off to the campsite. Arriving at the campsite, we were delighted to discover that my dad was there in the car park waiting for us, along with my

Uncle Roger. What a lovely surprise! My dear old dad, who had taken a keen interest in our progress, had driven almost five hundred miles just to see us. I'm so grateful for his support and encouragement of me throughout this whole venture. He'll never realise just how wonderful it was for us to see familiar friendly faces at this point in the trip.

After hasty tent erection, a quick shower and change of clothes, they scooped us up and treated us to a hearty meal before settling down in a local bar to watch England play against Italy in the Euros football final. Even though England lost the match (causing a great deal of cheering from the locals along with Italian music blasting from open windows!), it was still a great evening. We were still smiling as we crawled through the drizzle into our cold damp tent. Nothing could dampen our spirits: tomorrow would be the day we would finish the West Highland Way!

Day Twenty-Three:

The next day started with us losing things. Firstly, Allan's mobile phone simply disappeared whilst we were clearing up camp then we mislaid the path we were supposed to be following! We had unknowingly set off in completely the wrong direction and had walked about half an hour or so before we realised what we'd done.

Retracing our steps, we passed the campsite again before finding the correct path. We then enjoyed a gentle stroll along flat, leafy lanes towards Milngavie (pronounced 'mull-gai'), which marked the start (or for us the end) of the West Highland Way. There was only one hill to climb today and a lovely country park to walk through at the end which followed Allender Water right into the heart of the town.

This should have been a breeze for us but about two miles before the end, I suddenly felt weak and nauseous. I am not sure what happened but I had to sit down, rest for a bit and take in some calories and fluids before continuing to the end of the trail. On reaching the end, we took the obligatory photos and celebrated our achievement. We had completed the West Highland Way – a route attempted by many but finished by few. And we were OLD compared to the majority of folk who undertake it.

This was definitely a high point of our trip.

Chapter 8 – The Kindness of Strangers

Day Twenty-Five:

After a relaxing and restful day off in Glasgow, we turned our steps towards home and headed south. This was a new phase of our walk – we had said goodbye to the impressive wild Highlands of Scotland and were now making our way through the Lowlands towards the English border. Breath taking scenery had been replaced by grimy city streets, billboards screaming for attention and row upon row of practically identical houses. Goodness – I never realised quite how many people there are living in this land. It seemed a bit of a shock after all the isolation we'd enjoyed. But the urban landscape did make for an interesting walk through the suburbs that day – there was so much to see and take in. It certainly wasn't boring.

Leaving East Kilbride, south of Glasgow, we found ourselves walking along the side of a busy A-road before turning off to follow some quiet country lanes. It was sunny and hot. Walking on tarmac was tiring and hard on the feet. I think that having had a day off made it all the harder to get going again in some ways. Also, this was the first day of carrying our packs again after a full week of walking without them. It was going to take some getting used to again.

Some twenty miles after setting off, we arrived at the village of Strathaven, where we were staying. Just as we arrived, my arm vibrated, and my Garmin forerunner alerted me to the fact that I'd reached my step goal - we'd walked some 40 000 steps that day already! It's no wonder that we were both very tired. However, our old friend Cheesy Mashed Potato was back to greet us that night before we both fell exhaustedly into a deep slumber.

Day Twenty-Six:

The next day was a scorcher! Allan was really struggling at this point of the hike – his feet were very sore from burst blisters and that twisted ankle he'd suffered from a few days before was causing discomfort. It was difficult lugging heavy packs around and the heat was extremely challenging to contend with. Moaning and groaning, threatening to quit at the next town – he was not easy to cajole along. I truly thought that at this point he would give up and return home leaving me to complete the walk alone. I wasn't too concerned about that as originally, I had planned this as a solo venture and was mentally prepared to go it alone.

Eventually we made it as far as the almost unpronounceable town of Lesmagahow, where we found a lovely little café for lunch and spent some time resting in the shade of a tree in the local park. After some discussion, Allan agreed to walk as far as the English border with me before returning home to Hampshire. With this decision in mind, we continued our walk.

I'm not entirely sure who in their wisdom decided to name this part of the country the Lowlands but low it was not! Hill after hill faced us as we trudged wearily along laden down with heavy rucksacks. It was hard going! As we faced yet another daunting rise, we were greeted by a guy washing his car outside his house. We stopped to chat, glad of the brief respite, and were delighted to be offered ice-cold cans of Irn Bru to help us on our way: a carbonated soft drink of acquired taste produced here in Lanarkshire, originally as an alternative to alcohol for the steel workers to drink.

Donald was one of the friendliest and most hospitable people we had the pleasure of meeting, and we had a great chat. Feeling suitably refreshed, we continued on our way tackling each hill with ease. Sugar and drinks, as we were learning, were essential providers of the energy we needed for this walk. In fact, it's probably fair to say that most of our hill climbing was powered by jelly babies! A few jelly babies before tackling a big climb made all the difference in the world.

Walking along the deserted country roads, we were intrigued to spot a Portaloo on the roadside, with no sign of any sort of construction taking place nearby. On closer inspection, we discovered that this apparent toilet was in fact a library! It was fitted out with row upon row of shelves, crammed with books of all kinds. It had been re-purposed and was serving a valuable function for the entertainment of the locals. As an avid reader myself, I was encouraged by this sign of literary thirst in the midst of this somewhat remote community.

The day brought more pleasant surprises. A short while after the library, we walked past an old Victorian schoolhouse, where an elderly gentleman was painting the fence. We got chatting (as people were few and far between in these parts it was nice to exchange pleasantries with everyone we passed). On hearing of our venture, he invited us to stop for a cuppa. We spent a very pleasant hour or so chatting to the man and his lovely wife, who not only supplied cups of tea, but also fresh strawberries grown in the garden and a very Scottish treat – Tunnocks Caramel Logs (very sweet caramel filled wafer biscuits).

They told us all about the strange local custom of 'Boogie Racing', in which it seems you take your life in your hands as you career downhill at great speed in some kind of brakeless go-cart. It all seemed terribly dangerous to me, and I wasn't surprised to learn that in fact it had been banned due to a fatality that had occurred in the recent past. This couple also spoke of the village Olympics which are regularly held around these parts. This village was a hub for all kinds of activities. There was more community spirit and life around these quiet villages than I'd experienced in all my time living in a bustling market town in Hampshire. As we prepared to go on our way, they insisted on taking photos to put in the local newsletter – we were now famous (well, in this small part of the world anyway!)

A very pleasant evening was spent at Station House bed and breakfast in Lanark, where the lovely hosts gave us free wine and beer to enjoy with our evening meal. In fact, the owner also gave Allan six bottles of local ale to take on his journey with him the next day – quite tricky to carry six glass beer bottles on top of all the hiking equipment but Allan graciously accepted the gift.

Fortunately, whilst we were there, we were surprised to receive a phone call on the B & B landline from Donald, who we had met earlier in the day. He kindly offered to pick up our heavy rucksacks and transport them to the place we would be staying the following night. Kindness upon kindness that day worked its magic and helped to make Allan feel a bit more positive about the walk.

Day Twenty-Seven:

What a glorious feeling of freedom as we walked the following day without being lumbered down with those uncomfortable and cumbersome packs! Following quiet country roads before heading across open moorland was simply delightful, made all the better by finding a lone bench mid-way across the moor. Although it was another hot day, there was a pleasant breeze making the heat more bearable. At one point we found ourselves walking past fields of livestock with their accompanying horseflies (or 'clegs' as they are called in Scotland), where we had to keep moving fast and wave our arms around like mad things to try and avoid them.

The horsefly is an extraordinary creature, with excellent hunting abilities. Their primary sense for locating a suitable prey is the sense of sight and to that end, they have large compound eyes that serve this purpose well. They are attracted to large, dark objects (such as horses, cows or us!), to certain animal odours and carbon dioxide (which of course we humans emit as we breathe out) and to motion (and by simply walking along, we were moving of course). We were the perfect prey for them that day!

Horseflies, I discovered are very different to midges. For a start, they come in ones or twos rather than travelling around in great clouds; they follow you around and move faster than the average person – it's difficult to get rid of them simply by walking faster; they give you a nasty bite even through layers of clothing so covering arms and legs is not an effective defence against them;

finally, their bites are awful – red, swollen, painful and intensely itchy and what's more, they last for days. Unfortunately, we received quite a few nasty bites that day, even through multiple layers of clothing!

But even the horseflies couldn't dampen our spirits. Today was a good day for walking through the beautiful Scottish lowland countryside. We stopped briefly to chat to a young English couple, renovating a house in the picturesque village of Roberton, before making our way towards the M74, the route of which we would mainly follow all the way down to the English border as there is a minor road with a footpath running parallel to the motorway at this point. Our newly acquainted friend Donald was there to meet us at the service station where we would spend the night, with our heavy rucksacks in the boot of his car.

Having retrieved our baggage, thanked Donald profusely and checked into the hotel, we decided to catch the bus into the nearby town of Abington where we could get some supplies for the following day. Abington was disappointing. Although it boasts of hotels, cafes, and coffee shops, these were all closed on that particular day. There was nothing open except one small convenience store. We got what we could and retired to bed.

I was looking forward to the next day as a treat awaited us at the end of it. My mum's cousins lived nearby in the village of Canonbie. One of them, Howard, had offered not only to host us for a few days but also to run us back and forth from our start and finish points each day. That would take us as far as the English border, with home cooked food to look forward to, a comfortable bed, great company and no need to carry our packs for the next three days!

Day Twenty-Eight:

The following day started badly. After walking the first two miles, I realised that I'd left my trusty walking poles behind but with a full eighteen miles to walk that day, I didn't feel that it was worth adding an extra four miles to the trek in order to retrieve them. So, with regret, I came to a point of acceptance that they were gone. I reasoned to myself that they had done their job and seen me through the roughest terrain we were likely to face on the trip. I'd escaped without injury thus far and the walking should get easier from now on.

After looking at the route we were to follow, Allan, who was still struggling with his ankle, moaned about the amount of road walking we were due to do that day and he also voiced his disappointment that we wouldn't pass through the town of Moffat for which he seemed to have a particular, inexplicable fondness. Our exchanges became heated until finally a frosty truce ensued. We walked in silence, separated by more than the physical distance between us.

I found myself swinging between wishing that he would leave me to finish the walk alone and return home (it would be far less stressful than having him moaning and whingeing all the time after all) and hoping he would stay. I did really appreciate his support and admired the easy way he has of being able to talk to complete strangers. Also, it seemed to me that we'd had some amazing adventures together so far on this trip and I wanted to share more of them with him.

It's far too easy in life to get caught up in work, running errands or focussing on the needs of kids or elderly relatives at the expense of our most precious relationships. This was the most amount of time we had ever spent with each other in one go despite being married for thirty years. It was good for our relationship and deepened the bond between us. In truth, I would miss him terribly if he went home.

Although the road we followed ran parallel to the M74 motorway, it was surprisingly peaceful. Rich vegetation shielded us from the noise of the traffic. The road we were walking along was quiet with hardly any traffic and there was a good footpath to follow. The only trouble was that we were very exposed to the baking sun as Scotland's heatwave continued. It was hot and hard going. The intense sun bearing down on us sapped our strength and made for a challenging walk that day.

At one point, a passing cyclist stopped to chat to us – a teacher like me. He was from Gloucester and was cycling up to John O Groats from Land's End, not for charity but for a sense of achievement and self-fulfilment. We chatted about audiobooks and the absolute joy they are when you are travelling long distances as we were. You can forget your troubles and escape into another world completely when you have an audiobook to listen to. I enjoyed travelling to the great American plains, to the richness of India and to the war-torn land of Syria. I travelled back in time to the Elizabethan era and forward to some futuristic imagined world. I shared the lives of those who achieved great things, I wept with those who suffered, and I grew angry at the injustice faced by others. All of this through the amazing world of audiobooks!

After some fourteen miles of dragging ourselves through the intense heat and struggling under the weight of our packs, we took the decision to phone Howard and ask him to collect us sooner than we'd originally planned. Although it was only two O' clock in the afternoon, it made sense to walk fewer miles that day and make them up the following day when we wouldn't have to carry the packs at all.

Once our guardian angel in the form of my mum's cousin Howard arrived to rescue us, the day was transformed into a box of delights. After cool showers, clean clothes, and a good meal, we felt a whole lot better.

Day Twenty-Nine:

Walking jauntily along the next day, I found myself smiling - this was heaven compared to yesterday's struggle. The sun was shining, the sky was blue and cloudless, and everything seemed to be bathed in a shimmering light. We easily made up for the miles lost the day before and everything seemed effortless, helped by the fact that we only had light day packs to carry. We were accompanied by Gaye, one of the Scottish cousins (who was filling us in on some of the juiciest details of family history) who was walking with us for part of the day.

Howard was supporting us by regularly meeting us along the route with a cool box in the boot of his car, filled with cans of ice-cold drinks and tempting snacks to help us on our way. We made excellent progress and had finished before we knew it. As an added bonus, at the end of a day spent walking eighteen miles, we still felt energised, and our feet didn't even ache! Feeling encouraged, Allan took the decision to continue the walk with me.

Tomorrow would be a momentous milestone – we would finally reach the English border!

**

Day Thirty:

Lockerbie. To anyone over the age of fifty, the very mention of the word brings a feeling of sorrow. Of intense sadness. Of loss. The next morning started with a brief visit to the quiet village of Lockerbie in the Scottish borders before we started our walking for the day. This seemingly insignificant settlement was once the setting of a terrible and tragic disaster.

Shortly after 7pm on 21 December 1988, it was a scene of horror. Pan Am Flight 103, a transatlantic flight from Frankfurt to Detroit, was destroyed mid-flight by a bomb that had been covertly planted on board, killing all 243 passengers and 16 crew. Body parts and aircraft debris were catapulted to the ground all around this sleepy village, killing eleven local residents in the process.

Life for so many was cut short and for those unfortunate enough to have been living here at the time, life would never be the same – their own lives, although spared, were shaped and scarred by terrible sights. They carried memories that could never be forgotten. This small insignificant village in the heart of the Scottish borders was in an instant plunged forever into notoriety. Now everybody has heard of Lockerbie.

We spent some time wandering around the memorial ground, reading the plaques and stories associated with the tragedy. Young men and women, siblings, children and entire families wiped out in an instant. All their hopes and dreams, worries and concerns erased forever. All that potential dashed in a split second. It was a moving experience, made all the more intense by sharing the visit with Howard and Gaye who remembered the time and the impact on local people. They told us stories of local people who had themselves been directly affected by the tragedy. I will never forget my visit to Lockerbie.

Several hours later, arriving in the small village of Ecclefechan, famous for being the birthplace of Thomas Carlyle (who is said to be the founding father of fascism and a great influence on Hitler), we stopped briefly in the park before making our way towards the Solway Firth, where we enjoyed stunning views of the Cumbrian Lake District just across the water. At this point, England was so tantalisingly close to us.

We finished the day in Gretna Green, famous for weddings. This dates all the way back to the Clandestine Marriages Act of 1753, which prevented couples under the age of 21 marrying in England or Wales without their parents' consent. As it was still legal in Scotland to marry under the age of twenty-one without such consent, couples began crossing the border from England into Scotland to get married legally. The law may have long changed but Gretna's reputation as an ideal wedding location remains to this day.

From endings at the start of the day to beginnings at the end, I was struck by the brevity of life. None of us know what is round the corner for us or what the next day might bring. Everything can change in an instant. But still mankind lives with hope, makes plans, falls in love, lives life.

And that's the secret to contentment, I think. Not to be concerned with what has already happened – you can't change the past so there's no point dwelling on it. Let go of regret. But also, there's no merit in looking too far ahead, always longing for some future, better time that may never come to pass. Instead, we should learn to live in the here and now; take each day as it comes; be fully present; be grateful for each moment you have. Look around you and savour the experience of just being alive!

Day Thirty-One:

The following day was momentous. We had set off early as we knew it would be another very hot day. Howard dropped us off at our previous day's stopping point in Gretna Green and after only a couple of miles, we reached the English border. As we stood there, for our photoshoot with the famous 'Welcome to England' sign, a great sense of achievement hit us and we realised that in the past month, we had walked the entire length of Scotland. Not bad for an ordinary middle-aged couple from suburbia.

Just England left to go now.

Chapter 9 - Wild and Free!

The northernmost counties of England are truly special. Spacious, marked by wilderness and relatively unpopulated. It was a great experience to walk through this part of the country. This section of our trip was really enjoyable. For the next week, we skirted around the counties of Cumbria, Yorkshire and Lancashire, crossing from one to another again and again. All of them beautiful. All of them special.

That first day of walking through England was a delightful experience. We had set out early as we knew we had a hot day ahead of us. Initially, we continued following a path that ran parallel to the motorway before heading off and following a walkway through the Kingmoor Nature Reserve, leading straight into the heart of Carlisle. Green, leafy, shaded paths, free from traffic and practically deserted. It was a perfect start to the day.

The path emerged in an industrial estate on the outskirts of the city at which point, we got a bit lost. Fortunately for us, an elderly gentleman noticed our predicament and helped us out. He led us through the maze of factories and houses and showed us clearly the direction we should take. Then, having decided we were harmless enough, he invited us to his house for a cup of tea. What followed was a congenial half-hour or so of pleasant conversation with Ray, who turned out to be a fellow Jesus-follower. His wife had passed away just a few months before our visit, and I think he was pleased to have some company that day. It felt like another one of those 'meant-to-be' God encounters that we were becoming familiar with on this trip.

We followed the route he had indicated into the heart of Carlisle, walking alongside the river and through the Japanese Garden until, what seemed like, no time at all, we found ourselves at our first official stopping point for the day – a house belonging to distant relative of mine who lived in the city. Gemma, Cousin Gaye's daughter in law, was expecting us and welcomed us to her home with open arms. We stayed for a few hours, which spared us from walking through the hottest part of that sweltering day and enjoyed getting to know Gemma and her lovely children as well as spending more time with Gaye and her husband Raymond who had come over to meet us there.

On leaving Gemma's, we walked through Carlisle, briefly visiting the cathedral on the way, before making our way to Carleton, south of the city, where Howard was waiting to whisk us away for the last time back to his house in Canonbie. It had been great to see the Scottish side of the family and hear stories of my mum, my granny, my aunties and uncles. I learned a thing or two about some of the scandals they'd been involved in over the years – quite an eye-opener! Additionally, we'd been able to walk without packs and return at the end of each day to a home cooked meal, hot shower and a proper bed. We were intensely grateful for the hospitality we received.

Tomorrow would be a different story – carrying packs through the heat of the day and setting up camp once again at the end of the day. I was not looking forward to that prospect but knew that we couldn't stay where we were forever if our mission was to be accomplished and although it was a nice dream, it wouldn't be practical for Howard to continue driving ever increasing distances to ferry us back and forth at the beginning and end of each day.

So, grateful and energised from our 'oasis in the desert', we braced ourselves for what lay ahead.

Day Thirty-Two:

We were on our own again, carrying those dreaded packs once more. It was another very hot day, so we set off very early to walk the fifteen miles into Penrith from Carleton. Walking alongside the A6, we found there wasn't much shade, but the path afforded great views of the surrounding countryside and the Cumbrian hills beyond. After a brief stop in the quiet country churchyard of Plumpton, we made our way into the town of Penrith.

By the time we arrived, it was a very hot and humid twenty-eight degrees. Finding a cool and friendly café, we had some lunch and then parted company for a brief while. I spent some time crashed out in the shade under the yew trees of Saint Andrew's church, waiting for the intense midday heat to pass, whilst Allan wandered around the town, looking around the charity shops for bargains. This was his habit, and very much enjoyed browsing through all the CDs, books and vinyls on offer. Unfortunately, his browsing often led to purchases (he can't resist a bargain) and he ended up adding pounds of extra weight to his pack as the trip went on.

Eventually, we started off again, making our way through the south of the town, across several busy road junctions and walking the two and a half miles further on to the campsite where we were booked for the night. At one of the junctions, I spotted Allan, who had gone on ahead of me, walking in completely the wrong direction towards the town of Keswick – he was heading west instead of south! I tried phoning him but he wasn't picking up so I had to pursue him as fast as I could and wait for him to turn around so I could wave him back towards me. Eventually, he looked in my direction, noticed me wildly gesticulating to him and retraced his steps before we continued in the right direction once again.

Passing the site of King Arthur's Round Table, a Neolithic henge with a Celtic cross, we paused briefly to look around before continuing to Lowther Castle campsite, where the campsite receptionist gave us a generous donation before showing us to our pitch. She informed us that we had been upgraded at no extra cost to a serviced pitch (with electricity). Not much use to us though – we had nothing to plug in except mobile phones and no connectors for the power either. We collapsed on the grass, exhausted from the extreme heat and took a few minutes to catch our breath before setting up camp.

It's amazing how quickly our level of fitness had deteriorated. After just a few days of not having to carry all that weight around, we were struggling once again. Lying in the tent that evening, studying the route and the weather forecast for the following day, I was dismayed to see that the temperature was set to increase even more. It could reach thirty degrees tomorrow. Ugh....the prospect did not fill me with joy.

Day Thirty-Three:

Quite unexpectedly, the following day turned out to be rather special. Not the day I was dreading at all but instead, surprisingly pleasant! Expecting the day to get hot quite quickly, we'd packed up camp and were on the road not long after 6.30am. Walking through the deserted Lowther Castle estate, to the accompaniment of birdsong and babbling brooks, was a lovely and peaceful way to start the day. Re-joining our old 'friend', the A6, we followed it to the village of Shap, at which point we decided it was time for a coffee stop.

Entering the cool coffee shop, we looked around for somewhere to sit. The place was quite busy, with couples sat at tables and in one corner, a group of friends gathered for some sort of celebration. On one table, a solitary man sat enjoying his meal. He looked familiar but I couldn't quite place him. Where did I know him from? Spotting an empty table at the back of the shop, we took off our packs and ordered some food.

As we did so, the man stood up and came over to us. "Debbie and Allan? You've done well to get all the way down here!" In an instant, the penny dropped – this was Richard, the man we had met previously on the West Highland Way and given pills for his upset tummy. What were the chances of that? Here we were in the middle of nowhere and so was he – in the same coffee shop on the same day at the same time as us - what a coincidence! It turned out that his wife was the proprietor of this particular coffee shop which had only opened at the beginning of that week. Amazing. We had a good chat and afterwards, his lovely wife sent us away with home-made parkin and filled our water bottles with ice cold water for the journey.

Although the next seven miles were hot, they were pleasant as at this point we left the busy A6 and headed off across the moor to the village of Orton. The village had a shop selling ice-creams so we popped in. The lady running the village store was fascinated to hear of our adventure and made a generous cash donation to the charity. From Orton, it was less than two miles to the campsite, and we walked along tree-lined lanes to arrive by three o clock in the afternoon. Plenty of time then to relax and rest under the cool trees for the rest of the day.

***

Day Thirty-Four:

Ethereal. Mystical. Hushed. As we emerged the next morning from our tent, we were greeted by the magical sight of mist rolling down the nearby hills in great billows. Everything was muted. Dew covered the ground. All was still. It was as if we had left the real world behind and entered a mythical kingdom: one in which the regular rules of space and time no longer applied. I almost expected to spot a fairy or an elf among the trees. As we began to pack up camp, the mist gradually cleared and by the time we left, everything had once again returned to normal.

I think that starting the day with this dream-like experience had the knock-on effect of heightening my senses that day as we walked. I found myself noticing things around me with much greater attention than before: the sound of crickets, the smell of crushed grass as a tractor passed us, the wonderful sight of such a variety of colourful wildflowers on the roadside. Although it was an extremely hot day with many hills to tackle, it was delightful walking along the quiet country roads towards the town of Sedburgh. It was special eating our lunch in a quiet country churchyard (pitta bread with tuna packets and mini peppers was our usual fare as it was lightweight and compact as well as remaining fresh. Much better than eating soggy, squashed, warm sandwiches).

After lunch we set off again and continued through the open moorland until reaching Sedburgh – described on the sign welcoming us to the town as 'a place to breathe' - nestled between the Yorkshire Dales and the Lake District. It was nice to simply wander around the town for a while, one at a time whilst the other sat on a bench with the packs. The afternoon brought more blessings as we found ourselves walking alongside the river Lune. It was a very hot day – what could be nicer than plunging four feet for a while into the icy cold water? Allan took the opportunity to cool off with a swim. Eventually we arrived at our campsite for the night, Holme Farm, and were delighted to discover that the campsite had its own onsite café, selling freshly made pizzas. That was dinner sorted!

Day Thirty-Five:

The following day proved to be just as lovely. Apart from a brief spell of hiking alongside the A65 with no footpath, which was stressful and difficult, it was a good day. The weather was considerably cooler with a good amount of cloud cover and a refreshing breeze. Turning off the A65, we found ourselves in the pretty village centre of Ingleton, a beautiful Yorkshire Dales village nestled on the lower slopes of Ingleborough, one of Yorkshire's famous Three Peaks. We were somewhat surprised and a bit disappointed to find that it was a complete honey pot for tourists.

The place was crawling with visitors, drawn here by the famous waterfalls and caves. We discovered that it costs a whopping £8 per person to visit the waterfalls - by this time we'd seen so many beautiful waterfalls and hadn't had to pay a penny to see any of them! Spotting the church, we swiftly we took refuge in the quiet churchyard to eat our packed lunch but just as we started eating, a wedding party emerged from the chapel, and we were right in the way of the photographer. Beating a hasty retreat, we decided to just continue on our way. Quite honestly, we were glad to leave the place. Far too busy in late July for solitary hikers like us.

Arriving in the village of Clapham, we were delighted to find a village fair taking place in the churchyard. By now, it was quite late in the afternoon, and this worked to our advantage as the lovely ladies of Clapham gave us the leftovers from the home baked cake stall. Delicious. Clapham was much quieter than Ingleton and quite lovely. It is adjacent to the Ingleborough Nature Trail and cave walk, which did look beautiful, although after walking eighteen miles that day, I wasn't too keen to undertake it at that point. Allan thought he might start tomorrow by visiting the site. I simply added it to my mental 'must come back to' list!

***

Day Thirty-Six:

Walking through the wild expanse of open moorland the next day, I was struck by the incredible beauty of the scene, a landscape marked by grandeur and isolation. Vast open space spread out in all directions around us as we walked through the magnificent Forest of Bowland, designated as an official Area of Outstanding Natural Beauty. I could see how it earned this title. With fells rising in every direction, the heather coated moorland created a soft carpet on which sheep and cattle wandered freely, grazing amiably side by side. Above us, peregrines circled and soared on currents of air. The scene was enhanced even more by the gritstone boulders scatted seemingly randomly throughout the moor, their strength and solidity contrasting sharply with the soft, luxurious vegetation coating the land.

It was breath-taking. Even the numerous steep hills couldn't dampen our spirits. We felt free and alive. In fact, reaching the top of each incline brought greater pleasure as each peak afforded such magnificent views. Intending to stop for lunch in the vicinity of the Stocks Reservoir, we made our way downhill, picking wild berries as we walked.

The reservoir was something of a disappointment, rather non-descript and uninteresting, although we did discover that it was once the site of submerged villages which were gradually being uncovered by archaeologists. There wasn't much to see though apart from rather an abundance of midges who seemed intent on making us their lunch!

The afternoon proved hard. It was hot and muggy that day. Allan moaned and moaned and moaned. His feet hurt, his legs ached, he had bug bites, he was thirsty, hungry, tired, hot etc. On and on he grumbled. Looking back, I do have some sympathy as he did start the day by visiting the aforementioned nature trail and had probably walked a good three miles already before we had set off that morning. As well as that, we hadn't set off until ten o clock, which was a very late start for us and meant that we would not arrive at the campsite until early evening, making it a very long day. It was hot, we hadn't found anywhere to properly rest, and we hadn't had much to eat.

Finally, at about quarter to five in the afternoon, we came across a garden centre serving teas and coffees. Grateful for a chance to finally sit down and enjoy a cuppa, we stopped and took a break. We were their last customers of the day and by far the most appreciative, I'm sure!

From there, it was only a short distance to the campsite. Feeling suitably refreshed, we made our way there and quickly set up camp. Everyone we came across at the campsite was lovely. We seemed to generate interest wherever we went simply by the fact that we arrived without a car, carrying enormous packs on our back and we didn't fit the age profile of the average backpacker. All were interested to hear about our trip and our fundraising efforts for the Teenage Cancer Trust.

The farmer owning the field on which we were camping had been affected by cancer, losing his own father to the disease when he was just five years old. He generously waived our campsite fees and wished us well. A couple in the adjacent tent, having overheard the conversation, came over and gave us a cash donation. This was not an unusual occurrence by now. People were kind and caring. They wanted to donate to a worthy cause. We found that we regularly had to send money home to be banked throughout the trip. My faith in the innate goodness of humanity was being restored.

Later that evening, despite aching limbs and sore feet, it didn't take long to fall soundly asleep in a state of utter exhaustion. I was looking forward to not having to set up camp the following night.

Chapter 10 – The Industrial North

Day Thirty-Seven:

The following day marked the beginning of a new phase of the journey for us. Instead of camping each night, we had a series of cheap roadside hotels booked and would now be mainly hopping from city to city as we made our way steadily down the country. There would now be plenty of shops, cafes, and other such signs of civilisation along the way. Life should get a whole lot easier from now on.

As I sat enjoying the mouth-watering aroma of sizzling bacon whilst sipping my freshly roasted coffee, I was grateful for the abundance of places to eat. The day had started with a relatively short walk into the pretty market town of Clitheroe, where we found ourselves spoilt for choice of cafes offering inexpensive cooked breakfasts. The particular café we selected wasn't pretentious or fancy but offered a good deal. I am so glad we chose well as along with our breakfasts, we were presented with a very generous cash donation to the Teenage Cancer Trust from the staff working there, all of whom had given money to our cause. I was touched that even in this town, which didn't seem at all well off, people had hearts of gold and were eager to help those in need.

It was just as well that we'd fully refuelled that morning with a good breakfast, as the day proved to be quite a challenge physically.

I staggered on, sweat running off me in rivulets. Up and up and up we climbed. The road was getting increasingly steeper as we rose higher and higher. The seemingly endless climb was relentless. It was hard to keep on climbing but it was the way we needed to go. There was no other option. At one point, we passed by a dry-stone wall, so Allan decided to sit for a while and rest his legs.

"Get off my wall!" a voice exclaimed, seemingly out of nowhere. Following the sound of the voice, we spotted an elderly gentleman crouched down behind the wall, a large pile of rocks at his feet. Taking time, he patiently explained that he was repairing the dry-stone wall and he proceeded to go into some detail about what was involved. It was quite a skill. He voiced his concerns that dry-stone walling was a dying art as many young people were simply not interested enough to learn how to do it. It required patience and dedication to create such a masterpiece that would withstand the harsh weather conditions out here.

After our conversation, we walked on with greater respect and appreciation of these boundaries marking out the countryside around us. As we continued to climb, we found ourselves passing a sign on the roadside which read, 'Ski Centre'. That was all the confirmation I needed that this was quite a hill!

This was in fact the infamous Pendle Hill.

Rising 557 metres above sea level, Pendle Hill, part of the Pennine chain of hills and mountains, towers over the surrounding landscape. It's famous for two main reasons: firstly, in 1552 a man by the name of George Fox climbed Pendle Hill and had a vision which led to him founding a religious movement known as The Quakers. Secondly, it was known for the notorious seventeenth century witch trials which had been held here. Nine local women, known as the Pendle Witches, were tried, found guilty and hanged on 20th August 1612.

How ironic that this particular hill was associated with such extremes of both evil and goodness. Truly, it was a spiritual place, a place the mystics would call a 'thin' place: that is a place where the veil between this world and the eternal world is fragile, giving an awareness of both worlds coexisting simultaneously.

I could feel it.

Pausing at the top, grateful to finally have reached the peak, we noticed a memorial stone in honour of an Australian pilot, who died in 1942 and an American pilot whose plane had crashed there in 1944, just two years later. How very tragic. All in all, it was quite a sad place really but one with spectacular views across the Ribble Valley towards the Yorkshire Dales National Park.

Descending into the village of Sabden, which took hardly any time at all compared to the time it had taken to climb up the hill, we intended to stop for lunch but disappointingly, the entire village was closed – the pub, the café, the museum and even the village shop were all shut. Time after time we found this – places were still badly affected by the pandemic. Life in this post-pandemic world was not completely back to normal after all.

By this point in our walk, we'd become gloriously oblivious to what was happening in the world, including the progress of COVID-19 infections throughout the country. It was quite refreshing to have completely disconnected from the relentless stream of negative news which had bombarded us over the past couple of years. We may not have been up to date with the news, but as our experience in Sabden showed, we were still affected by it. So, after some time fruitlessly wandering around this seemingly dormant village, we had no choice but to just continue on our way. Leaving Sabden behind, another monster of a hill faced us. Ugh.

A word on hills......according to the Oxford English Dictionary, a hill is a "naturally raised area of land". They may all share the same definition, but as we discovered, not all hills are the same. Some have a steep incline; others are long with a lower gradient. Some are smooth and level; others bumpy or uneven. Whatever type of hill you are facing, it's always a challenge for the hiker carrying a fully laden pack on their back! When you are faced with yet another hill, you have to develop a way of dealing with them.

Everyone has their own way. I found the best way to tackle a steep climb was not to overthink it, but instead to distract myself by listening either to music or an audiobook. Then to simply take one step after another until it was done. 'Slow and steady wins the race' was my approach. Allan's approach was somewhat different from mine. He steamed up them, taking the view that the more quickly he climbed them, the better, as then they were over and done with. He often got time to rest and admire the view whilst I was still plodding my way steadily uphill. We did get used to climbing steep hills wearing fully laden rucksacks though and after a while they didn't seem like such a big deal – after surveying the prospect of a steep climb, we found ourselves saying, "It's just another hill."

As we walked that day, the scenery around us completely changed. We passed from beautiful open countryside to urban sprawl. Padiham, where we stopped for a drink, was run down. Boarded up shops, graffiti covered fences in disrepair, bottles, cans and packets littering the streets. One man told us that it wasn't the sort of place in which to hang out after dark. What I did notice was that out of all the convenience stores we passed, not one was selling fresh fruit or healthy snacks. The only offerings were crisps, chocolate, fizzy drinks, ready meals, and lottery tickets. I found this quite shocking and disturbing. Why are the choices on offer in some of our most deprived areas so limited? I know its demand driven – those are the things that the shopkeeper knows will sell well - but should it be the case? No wonder that health outcomes and life expectancy in these areas drop quite considerably.

In Burnley, we found the Travelodge and gratefully collapsed onto the bed. It had been a hard day today. I realised that I'd gotten quite sunburnt as I'd walked that day too. Oh well, I'd have a nice tan after all this exposure to the elements. We did some washing in the bath of the Travelodge, before hanging the essential items up to dry on the heated towel rail. This was a bit of an experiment, but it worked well as by the morning, everything had dried beautifully. This simple procedure was repeated pretty much every day from then on, giving us clean clothes to wear each day (especially important now that we were back in civilisation).

***

Day Thirty-Eight:

As we walked past a reservoir the next morning, a flood of memories and emotions came rushing back. A different reservoir (it may well have even been the same one), a different time, but still me and Allan walking on a dappled path beside the still, dark waters of the reservoir, under the rustling leaves. We were different people then – me an insecure young primary school teacher, him a handsome young Scotsman – on our very first official 'date'. Full of hopes and dreams, questions and uncertainties.

Actually, I'm still full of hopes and dreams, questions and uncertainties....maybe I am the same person after all. Just older, a bit wiser, a lot wearier and worn down by the world. That particular day, 27th July, was our 30th wedding anniversary. It seemed fitting that we should spend it walking through the part of the country where we'd had our very first date. How extraordinary that we would end the day in a Travelodge just three miles away from Heywood, where we had first met each other thirty-one years ago.

The walking that day was different – mostly on paved footpaths through various towns and villages. I found it quite interesting – a novelty – looking at gardens and buildings on the way. We passed through old mill towns and even at one point, passed beside a steam railway. For a short section, we found a picturesque off-road path beside a river to follow before re-joining the road. After one particularly steep climb, we stopped for a drink at a roadside café with amazing views of Bury. A kind couple, seeing us labouring up the hill through the intense heat, offered us a lift which we politely declined, explaining our mission. After settling into the Travelodge at Bury, we enjoyed an anniversary meal at the adjacent fast-food restaurant. Not exactly fine dining, but it made a nice change from rehydrated cheesy mashed potato and sardines!

Day Thirty-Nine:

Manchester. I wonder what image that word conjures up for you? For me, having always lived on the south coast, it brought images of industrial grime, polluted air, and rough living, not to mention violent crime. I was expecting to see numerous factories spewing venomous clouds of yellowy-black smoke, row upon row of back-to-back houses, tower block slums, drunkards and drug addicts roaming the streets, beggars clawing at me on every street corner. Gripping tightly onto the rucksack straps and keeping my head down, I was half expecting to be mugged or murdered on our walk through the city that day. I guess I'd had too much exposure to Dickens and to gritty TV dramas set up north!

My experience of Manchester was somewhat different and blew my expectations right out of the window.

Having left the hotel at 7.30am, we made our way through the suburbs towards the heart of the city. It was quite interesting seeing the wide variety of shops and businesses as we passed through Prestwich, then Salford. At one point we passed several high-end restaurants before plunging almost immediately into a very run-down area of the city. The contrast was intense. Here, we saw shop after shop selling identical goods – T shirts and fizzy drinks – each one with a middle eastern gentleman standing, seemingly on guard, outside the shop. "Ah," I thought in my somewhat naive and judgemental way, "*This* must be one of the 'dodgy' areas." Each seller tried in vain to get us to enter the shop and purchase their goods, pleading with us to enter. It was surreal!

Politely declining their pleas but not wanting to offend, we did at one point get drawn into conversation with one of them. Once we stopped to talk, it was as if we had some invisible magnetism. Within minutes we were completely surrounded by the men. They hovered around us like bees round a honey pot. I was alarmed. Was this it? Is this how it would all end? However, once again, my fears proved to be unfounded. I had mistaken their intentions. They were curious and genuinely interested in us and just wanted to find out what we were doing walking through the city wearing enormous heavy rucksacks on our backs. Fair question really. All of them wanted to be photographed with the two of us for their Instagram posts. They made us feel like celebrities.

Walking into the very heart of the city was delightful. It was vibrant, alive, and shiny! Not at all what I was expecting. There had obviously been quite a bit of investment in the city centre, and it was great. Arriving early, we had time to spare so we visited the cathedral, the art gallery and the museum. All were wonderful and it made a nice change for us to be proper tourists for a short while. The streets were full of young students; buskers were on every corner; shops seemed to be doing a roaring trade. At one point we came across an amazing area underneath the road system filled with picnic benches and graffiti-covered shipping containers selling a wide variety of street foods. We stopped for food here, joining the dozens of students doing the same. Quite a vibe!

Then, as we continued on our way, we experienced the most dramatic weather event of the entire trip. Walking along the streets, both musing quietly to ourselves under an increasingly gloomy sky, our thoughts were rudely interrupted by an almighty flash of light, closely followed by the deep, booming sound of thunder. Within moments the sky opened as if ripped in two by the lightning and a deluge of torrential rain immediately engulfed us. Rain hammered down on the road surface, ricocheting back up to soak us through from below as well as above. There was little hope for us of staying dry. It was futile trying to avoid the worst of it, although we found ourselves dashing from bus stop to bus stop in a vain attempt to do so. Drenched through from head to foot, we sprinted for cover in a fast-food café. As we entered, the staff immediately ran for the mops, trying in vain to prevent the Biblical scale flood which threatened to engulf both them and the other customers.

After that, we both bought umbrellas!

Day Forty:

The following day, having dried out sufficiently from yesterday's fiasco, we walked out of Manchester, crossed over the River Mersey and through the southern suburbs towards Macclesfield. Walking through the sleepy village of Handforth, south of Manchester, we were interested to discover that it once housed one of Britain's largest First World War Prisoner of War camps. From 1914 to 1919, thousands of men, mostly captured German soldiers but also Austro-Hungarian labourers, Croatian seamen and Polish soldiers, were interned there. Apart from various information boards along the route, very little evidence remained of its history. I wondered how many of this diverse group of people went on to settle in the area.

Later that morning, we found ourselves battling with traffic as we walked along a busy B-road, again with no footpath, until we reached the picturesque village of Prestbury. Eating our lunch sitting under the shade of a tree in the village park, we looked around. Everything looked pristine and very well to do. My first impressions were that this was quite a pretentious area – the cafes seemed vastly overpriced and the gift shops extortionate! Later, we discovered that Prestbury boasts of having the most expensive road to live on in the North of England and it's home to many famous footballers and celebrities. My first impressions had been correct!

From Prestbury we were able to walk along the Bollin Way,

following the River Bollin right into the heart of Macclesfield. The path was lovely, going through some beautiful countryside and frequented by lots of very friendly dog walkers, many of whom wanted to stop and chat. The medieval town of Macclesfield, once the heart of the silk industry, was a really nice end to the day. We spent some time wandering around the quaint town centre which was filled with antique shops, gift shops and cute cafes along with the usual range of shops found in every other town up and down the land.

I looked forward to the next phase of the trip. Tomorrow we would leave the busy roads and start to follow the canal network, which would take us through the midlands towards the heart of the Cotswolds.

Chapter 11 – Travelling along with Rosie and Jim

Peaceful. That's how I would describe the experience of following a canal towpath. There's nothing quite like it. Listening to crickets, birdsong, and gently rippling water. Feeling the cool shade of the trees and the soft breeze on your skin. Seeing the brightly painted barges slowly making their way through the still waters, cutting through the smooth, glassy surface like knives through butter. It was so restful. And what's more, it was level – no major hills or even steep slopes to contend with. Quite a change. Also, after dodging traffic for most of the previous day, it was relaxing to be able to walk without that feeling of hyper-vigilance all the time.

The jovial holiday makers traveling by barge were friendly. Many of them smiled and waved as they passed or were interested to talk to us and find out what we were up to. I suppose one reason for this being the fact that not much happens on a canal boat holiday. Apart from time spent contending with locks, it's an uneventful way to travel. Spotting an odd, middle-aged couple walking along with massive packs on their backs must have been quite an event for them. One family we passed even gave us tea and jam tarts as they passed by!

Day Forty-One:

The morning started with us walking along the Macclesfield Canal to Congleton, where we stopped briefly for lunch before resuming our walk along the same canal towards Stoke on Trent, stopping briefly at Kidsgrove for a super-refreshing drink in the garden of pub overlooking the canal. There are lots of lovely places to stop for refreshments and plenty of conveniently placed benches along the canal network which was great for us.

The only disadvantage of sticking closely to the canal network, was that we actually increased our milage quite considerably. Canals aren't always the most direct routes to follow. But we figured that the quality of the experience more than made up for the fact that we had to walk a few extra miles. That day, although we had planned to walk fifteen miles, we ended up walking about twenty miles or so. By the time we arrived in Stoke, we were bone-weary and ready for bed. Due to our utter exhaustion, it was once again back to cheesy mashed potatoes and sardines for dinner that night. Tired but contented, soon after arriving, we were fast asleep.

Day Forty-Two:

The following day began with a hair-raising walk along one of the busiest roads we'd encountered on our walk so far – a dual carriageway with no footpath, populated with vehicles desperately racing to get to their destinations with little regard for the poor hikers carefully picking their way along the kerbside. It was scary! Spotting a fast-food restaurant at the roundabout ahead of us, we decided to calm our nerves, look for another route and enjoy a brief interlude of rest before continuing. Having done a quick google search of alternative routes, we found a footpath really close to where we currently were, passing through some farmland which would give us some respite from the traffic.

We followed the route suggested and eventually found ourselves in the leafy suburbs of Newcastle Under Lyme. It was a typical Saturday morning in the sleepy suburbs – people out walking their dogs, children playing football in the park whilst their parents watched on supportively, ordinary folk going about their usual business, oblivious to the trauma we'd experienced that morning or the adventures we'd had previously.

From Newcastle Under Lyme, we followed the Trent and Mersey Canal towards Stafford. At this point I discovered that not all canals are alike. This canal was not the quiet, rural setting we had encountered yesterday on the Macclesfield canal or the tranquillity of the Caledonian Canal up in Scotland. No, this canal was very industrial and so much busier than we'd encountered before. Warehouses and factories lined the route, along with graffiti-covered bridges and tall chimneys, all pointing to the industrial heritage of the area.

We were now walking through the area of England known as 'The Potteries', named on account of the many potteries producing fine china in the area. In 1761, Josiah Wedgwood was instrumental in drawing up plans for a canal connecting Stoke-on-Trent, where his pottery was located, to the River Mersey, where the goods could be exported overseas. Transporting pots is a tricky business due to the fragile nature of the goods. He needed to find a way for the safe and smooth transport of his pots. Pots transported by road were likely to be damaged or broken so a canal was a better form of transport for these fragile goods. Hence, the Trent and Mersey Canal, alongside which we were currently walking, was formed.

We were grateful to such patriarchs of old for the chance to walk along level, paved footpaths away from the busy traffic of the cities. Information boards, giving details of the industrial heritage of the route, were located at regular intervals along the towpath, adding to the interest of the walk that day. We stopped at the pretty market town of Stone for lunch before continuing on our way. It was a pretty place, filled with quirky little shops and antique stores. On arriving in the town of Stafford, we stopped in the park for a bit, which had a music event taking place, with some excellent singers, before finding our hotel. All in all, it had been another good day.

***

The National Cycling Network was set up in 1995 with the aim of encouraging cycling and walking throughout Britain. It contains nearly 13 000 miles of signed routes, with over 5000 miles of those being completely traffic free. Yet another blessing for the long-distance hiker. The next day we found ourselves switching between canal walking and these cycle paths as we made our way towards Wolverhampton. We started by walking on a cycle path running adjacent to the A449, before joining the Staffordshire and Worcestershire canal. We stopped briefly for a short break in the village of Penkridge and then re-joined the cycle track once again. After a while, we found ourselves back on the canal towpath. We finished the day with a seemingly endless trek through the suburbs. The outskirts of Wolverhampton seemed to go on forever and towards the end of the day, we were feeling weary. Fortunately for us, before long, we passed an oasis of peace in the form of a garden centre.

Garden Centres are a truly British phenomenon. In all my travels to various parts of the world, I have never come across Garden Centres quite like the ones we have in this country. In most other places, Garden Centres sell plants and things needed for gardening but here in the UK, they are wonderful places selling not only plants but gifts, clothing, books, speciality food items and much more. At Christmas, they are transformed into vast light-filled grottos with animated displays and wonders galore. Truly a sight to behold.

For us, one of the best aspects of garden centres is that they are largely dry, spacious, comfortable and they serve tea! Furthermore, they have large trolleys, designed for carrying all the plants and other goods a customer wants to buy, but these trolleys are also great for carrying heavy rucksacks. Taking off the heavy packs for a while was bliss. We enjoyed a visit to the café before spending some time meandering around, looking at all the plants and gifts on offer. Eventually, we tore ourselves away, put on our heavy packs once more and walked on towards the hotel.

**

We heard it before we saw it: the rhythmic sound of traditional Indian music, quite unique, was flowing out from the open, lower hotel windows as we approached. Unfamiliar instruments of one sort or another were blending together to create a harmonious cacophony of Asian soundscape. We could hear laughter and conversation above the din. A joyous celebration was obviously taking place in the hotel this evening.

As we entered the hotel, it was as if we were whisked away on a magic carpet into another more exotic world. There were people wearing vibrant colours everywhere. Elegant pink saris, bejewelled purple saris, silky turquoise saris. So many beautiful costumes, all contributing to the joy of the occasion. It was awesome.

Then we saw her.

The bride. Looking spectacular in her ruby-red sari, embellished with fine embroidery, her hands bearing the beautiful, delicate markings of the henna patterns so carefully drawn. Sitting on a chair in the hotel lobby, she giggled conspiratorially, with her finely dressed friends. It quite took our breath away to witness this special moment in a young girl's life. But it did feel quite intrusive looking on the scene, so we retreated to the solitude of the hotel room, thankful to have been privileged enough to have seen it.

Day Forty-Three:

The next morning, having left bright and early, we made our way through the wonderful Baggeridge Country Park: a beautiful area of countryside on the edge of the Black Country. It was a nice mix of ancient woodland, marshland, signs of industrial heritage (it was formerly the Baggeridge Colliery) and 150 acres of parkland. There was even a large lake known as Bag Pond. Eventually, after walking through the park, we reached a large country house with a small outdoor café and we stopped for coffee. It was a nice start to the day. On leaving the park, we followed the A449, which had a good footpath alongside. This meant we were making good time and were hopeful of arriving at our destination in good time so we could enjoy a bit of a rest. That optimism however didn't last long.

The path we'd been happily following came to a sudden end and we found ourselves once again at the mercy of the traffic. The road was very fast and dangerous to walk on. Not good. Making swift use of the Ordinance Survey mapping App, we managed to find an off-road route. Gratefully, we headed away from the busy A449 and towards the open countryside. Although we were following an official right of way, it soon became apparent that the farmer didn't share our enthusiasm for public footpaths. The paths were overgrown with nettles and brambles, but we battled on like swashbuckling knights of old, slashing our way through deep jungles to rescue a damsel in distress.

Eventually the overgrown path gave way to open farmland. Swathes of corn stretched out in every direction, inviting us forward. Treading carefully on the ridges of soil between rows, the words of that well known song by Sting came to mind as we really did walk in fields of gold. Here we were together, just the two of us, on a sunny afternoon, in the heart of our adventure. Bliss.

After a while, we found ourselves on a farm track, where some workmen were busy renovating a small cottage. They asked where we were going, and on discovering what we were up to, they directed us to the canal towpath, giving us words of encouragement and telling us that we would receive a rich reward in heaven.

We followed the Stourbridge Canal to the canal basin in Stourton, where we met a family on one of the boats who came from the town of Eastleigh, about fifteen miles from our own hometown of Fareham in Hampshire. It was good to chat from folks back home. It felt in some strange way as if we were from the same tribe. After Stourton, we walked through some very hilly but picturesque villages before once again joining the A449, which thankfully now had a footpath running alongside it. Walking into Kidderminster, we passed beside an old waterwheel.

Kidderminster was run down and tired looking. What had once been a vibrant high-street was now a relic of times gone by. Gone were the busy department stores, the fashionable clothes shops, and the quirky independent retailers, replaced instead by discount stores, charity shops, tattoo studios and betting shops. Sadly, this was typical of the town centres we passed through on our travels. I guess the pandemic had hastened the switch to online retail, sounding the death knell for our High Streets up and down the land. On the edge of the town, beside the river, we found a cute little curry house and enjoyed sitting beside the river eating al fresco. It was a lovely way to end the day. Only one more walking day to go before our next day off. Can't wait!

Day Forty-Four:

The next day started in a way that was practically perfect; we awoke to clear blue skies, and we set off joyfully, anticipating our arrival later that day in Worcester which would herald the start of our next (and final) day off. By this time, we had been walking for three weeks solid, without a break, and we were looking forward to not only resting but also to catching up with one of our good friends, Karen, who was driving up to Worcester to meet us and would spend the day with us tomorrow.

Initially that day, we followed the canal towpath towards Stourport, leaving Kidderminster behind. The weather was good – sunny but not too hot. As we walked along, all was peaceful and calm. Everything had a quiet stillness about it, a sort of hush. It was a lovely way to start the day. Sort of grounding. We felt at peace and enjoyed the solitude of the early morning. No one was around – just us and the creatures of the natural world; birds, fish, insects. The geology was interesting here – vast orangey-brown sandstone cliffs bordered the canal, their forms reflected in the still waters of the canal. This provided a stunning backdrop to our walk that morning. Unhurried and undisturbed, we continued quietly along until we reached the town of Stourport.

After such tranquillity, the town of Stourport was a bit of a shock. It is described as a 'lively' town with 'vibrant' shopping streets. That seems a bit of an understatement – it was hectic! Full of traffic and people milling around, jostling us about and all in a hurry to get somewhere. We made our way through the town as quickly as our packs would allow, desperate to get out of the busyness and find the Severn Way, which we then planned to follow into Worcester.

The Severn Way was not what we expected. The Severn Way is a recognised long-distance walking route which follows the River Severn downstream from source to sea, passing through Wales, Shropshire, Worcestershire and Gloucestershire. We had naively assumed that as it is an officially recognised long distance walking path, it would be well maintained and easy to follow. We were mistaken. Nothing could be further from the truth. Instead, we found overgrown paths, broken fencing and a lack of way marker signs. It was not at all well maintained. To top it all, there was a distinct lack of view of the river itself.

After battling through miles of head-height, somewhat vicious stinging nettles, rough, tangled, and extremely prickly brambles and vines entangling us with their creepy tendrils, getting more than our fair share of nettle stings and bug bites, we found ourselves passing through a series of sheep fields, in which we had to tread carefully to avoid the rivets, clods and turds littering the ground. It was distinctly tricky! It was exhausting so as we approached the outskirts of Worcester, we decided to abandon the Severn Way we'd originally planned to use and instead follow the road into the city, which thankfully had a good footpath running alongside. Arriving in Worcester, we stopped for a while in one of the parks before making our way towards the Severn View Hotel where we would spend the next two nights.

Chapter 12 – No Longer Alone

The Severn View Hotel, with its romantic sounding name was not what we imagined it would be. An estate agent would probably describe it as 'rustic'. The room to which we were shown (after a brief interlude for the proprietor to find the mislaid room key) was large and airy with a good amount of natural light streaming in though the window. But the windows didn't shut properly and rattled continually, the plumbing was questionable, with extreme clunking sounds every time a tap was turned, there were stains on the carpet and the wallpaper was peeling off in places. However, as Allan pointed out to me, it was a step up from spending the night in a tent and having to set up and pack up camp each night. So, with resignation, I came to an acceptance that this was to be our 'home' for the next two nights.

Day Forty-Five:

Rising ridiculously early the next morning (why do our bodies do that to us when we have a day off?), I spent a surprisingly pleasant hour in the local laundrette as soon as it opened at 7am watching the grubby, foul-smelling damp garments that had been stuffed hurriedly into the rucksacks, tumble round and round as they morphed into fragrant, freshly laundered clothes. Quite a hypnotic and strangely satisfying start to the day!

Suitably clean and smelling as fresh as daisies, we met up with our good friend Karen Sage. She offered to take home anything we no longer needed on the trip to save us carrying it so we gratefully sent a truck load of stuff home (included all those Cds and books that Allan had been buying along the way!), putting it all in the back of Karen's car, and made straight for a local coffee shop. It was so nice to see a familiar face from home again. We spent the day catching up on news from home while wandering around the city, popping into shops, cafes, and touristy places.

Worcester is a lovely city to while away the time. Built on the River Severn, this beautiful city, with its impressive cathedral is home to all number of interesting sights: half-timbered buildings, museums and galleries, cafes and shops and wonderful riverside walks. It has it all and we loved making the most of the time we had there. At midday, Karen treated us to lunch in a vegan restaurant. This was a decision we lived to regret, but more on that later. It had been another fine day with sunshine throughout and we counted ourselves blessed to have had the opportunity to properly enjoy it.

Day Forty-Six:

The next day started well enough. We followed the path running alongside the river battling once again through endless tunnels of nettles and brambles before it became impossible to follow the official Severn Way. The route ahead of us was closed for maintenance, and we found ourselves following the diversion up and over the river to the other side. Confusedly, we looked around, trying to work out which way we should go as the signs were not very clear. Just then an elderly cyclist dismounted and stopped to chat. It turned out that he himself had cycled the entire Lands' End to John O Groats route twice in his lifetime. Pretty impressive! He advised us of a footpath we could follow that wouldn't take us too far off the route.

Taking his advice, we changed direction but found that it wasn't as straightforward as we'd anticipated. The new footpath was difficult to follow, and we found ourselves trekking straight across farmers' fields and down overgrown ditches. Eventually we made our way back onto the official Severn Way route, which took us straight through a large country estate, complete with Capability Brown lakes and horses. Leaving the estate, we walked through a series of towering maize-filled fields and once again found ourselves walking beside the river.

Unfortunately, the day just got worse and worse from that point on. Firstly, I lost Allan (again!). Unusually, I was actually ahead of him when I left the river to follow a small minor road that made up a part of the route. After about five minutes, I stopped walking and waited for him to join me. He never appeared. I waited some more. No Allan. Hmm. I retraced my steps back to the river, but he was nowhere to be found. Then it started to rain. Great. When my phone began to ring, I grabbed it and was relieved to hear his voice confusedly asking where I was. He'd completely missed the turning off the riverside path and had gone some considerable distance further along. Once we'd sorted that out and located each other again, we continued our way to the village pub, where we stopped for a lunchbreak.

The weather continued to deteriorate whilst we ate. It was raining hard by now. Pulling on our dripping coats and lifting our sodden packs once more, we set off along the road towards Tewkesbury. After a couple of miles, Allan's vegan meal from the previous day returned to haunt him. Feeling a sudden and irresistible urge to use a toilet, we picked up speed and headed for a truckers' café as indicated on google maps. We found it without too much trouble, but it was shut. Poor Allan. "Never mind," we thought, "there's a service station just up the road. They're bound to have a loo he can use." Racing up the road, we reached it just in time only to find that this particular service station had permanently closed shortly before we got there. Drat. Resignedly, Allan quickly headed for the nearby bushes, vowing never again to touch vegan food.

But that was not the end of our troubles that day.

Walking on the path alongside the main road into Tewkesbury was a mixed blessing. On the one hand it was direct and fast. However, there was one big problem with it. Due to the sheer volume of rain that day, there were many large puddles, which it seemed, every single car and lorry took delight in driving straight through with the single intention of splashing us to soak us through even more. By the time we reached the outskirts of the town we were dripping from every orifice possible. I'm sure it was amusing for them but not so much fun for us. Not a dry centimetre of us or our stuff remained. Soaked through from head to foot, we began to get very cold.

Passing a garden centre, we went inside with the intention of getting a warm cuppa to thaw us out a little bit. But you've guessed it, the café was shut even though the garden centre itself was still open. Seeing our crestfallen faces, one sympathetic member of staff took pity on us. She went into the staff room and made two cups of tea for us to drink before sending us on our way. It's these little, seemingly insignificant, kindnesses that I remember the most. Without such acts, I'm not sure we would have made it all the way to the end. They kept us going and lifted our spirits when the going got tough.

Eventually, we made it to Tewkesbury, found the hotel and gratefully poured ourselves through the door.

Entering the hotel, we were welcomed by a friendly member of staff, even though we were by this time completely soaked through and dripping all over the lobby floor. We were warmed by the sight of low beamed ceilings, heavily carpeted floors, wood panelling on the walls, a homely open fireplace and beautiful glass chandeliers hanging from the ceilings. The Tudor Inn Hotel was truly special, boasting many period features. This historic hotel has a rich history of which it was evidently very proud. As we made our way to the room, walking through the wonky corridors and ducking to avoid the low wooden ceiling beams, we passed many oil portraits of Tudor figures in gilt frames and even a complete suit of armour, complete with a menacing looking sword. The room was delightful with its solid dark oak furniture, rich tartan fabrics and an ensuite fully equipped bathroom. It was a great place to stay.

Day Forty-Seven:

Suitably refreshed from a good night's sleep and after a substantial breakfast in the hotel, we made our way through the picturesque town, stopping briefly at the Abbey on the way past. Tewkesbury is a wonderful town, full of history with its medieval buildings, Norman church tower and Tudor beamed houses. Nestled between the River Severn and the River Avon, its setting is perfect. We vowed to return to this lovely place in the not-too-distant future.

Returning to our nemesis, the Severn Way, we spent the morning walking through sheep fields and over many stiles (which are not easy to navigate when wearing a cumbersome, fully laden pack on your back!) loosely following the course of the river. We were a bit disappointed to find that we only had the occasional glimpse of the river through the trees; I had assumed we'd see a lot more of it than we did. However, when we did see the river, it was a bit of a let-down. Brown, murky water stretched out in both directions. It wasn't a particularly attractive river at all. Having stopped to chat with a group of ramblers, we were advised to abandon the Severn Way as it was about to become a lot harder to follow and unpleasant to walk along due to the build-up of industry along the river's edge. So, we decided at that point to change course and follow the roads, which fortunately all had footpaths we could walk on.

We passed through several villages until eventually reaching the city of Gloucester. Making straight for the hotel, we checked in and left our bags in the room before venturing out to explore the city. After passing through the usual city centre range of shops, we rounded a corner and caught our breath. Wow. The magnificent form of Gloucester Cathedral stood before us. Towering above the city buildings in a square of its own, this imposing gothic style church is a truly impressive structure.

Although the cathedral was closed to visitors, we were delighted to discover that the Evensong service was about to begin. We were just in time. Joining the trickle of people filing through the doors, we took our seats. As the melodic organ music soared and swooped around us, carried through the vast nave, I gazed up, captivated by the awe inspiring intricate and detailed carvings on the majestic sandstone walls and the delicately detailed stained-glass windows. It was very peaceful, and we felt privileged to have experienced the exquisite music of the gifted choristers.

***

Day Forty-Eight:

Making our way across the city early the next morning, we stopped briefly outside a fast-food restaurant, not for the purpose of getting breakfast but to meet up with our son Luke, his father-in-law Kevin and Dexter the dog. My heart filled with joy as I saw them there waiting expectantly for us. Today was going to be an excellent day; nothing would dampen my spirits today. I was certain of it. The plan was that Kevin and Dexter would walk along the Gloucester to Sharpness Canal with us for the day, while Luke supported us by transporting our packs, setting up the tent at the campsite and meeting up with us, providing suitable refreshments, at various intervals along the way.

The day simply flew by as we walked and chatted for mile after mile. There was so much to see. We had the canal to our left and the River Severn to our right, with impressive views of Wales beyond, looking moody with a covering of dark, menacing cloud. We passed many interesting things on the way. At one point I counted twenty separate fishermen, who had set up their rods and equipment along the Canalside! Intrigued, I asked if there was an abundance of fish in the vicinity but apparently that wasn't the case – in fact there was an angling competition that particular day and they were all keenly competing to win the prize.

At one point, somewhere near a village named Purton, we took a slight detour off the towpath to visit something intriguingly named 'The Ship's Graveyard'. Following the signposts down to the riverside, we came across the strange sight of a collection of abandoned boats of varying sizes, scattered along the shoreline. Nestled in amongst the reeds and mudflats, these decaying hulks, many of which were filled with concrete, had an almost ghostly appearance. By that time the weather was grey and overcast with a steady drizzle, making the experience of viewing the 'ghost ships' even more atmospheric. It really did appear to be a ship's graveyard.

We learned from the information boards that these historic boat wrecks had been deliberately beached here throughout the 20th century in an effort to protect the banks of the River Severn from eroding into the canal. Most were beached in the 1950s and, despite being filled with concrete, are now in a state of considerable decay. Although there are other such places, this site forms the largest ship graveyard in mainland Britain. It was an impressive sight and definitely worth the short detour.

The weather continued to deteriorate further as the day went on and by the time we neared the end, we were all completely drenched. Poor Kevin – we were used to being wet by now, but he had only joined us for the day. Cold, tired, and soaked through to the skin, we were relieved to finally come across Luke and his car at the end of the day's walk. We'd walked about nineteen miles that day and were ready for a rest. Unfortunately, we had to wait a little longer for our rest as something happened that caused us to stay put for a while.

After loading up the wet bags and the somewhat soggy doggy and piling gratefully into the car ourselves, we started out for the campsite we'd booked into for the night. Looking out of the steamy windows, hypnotised by the rhythmic sound of the wiper blades passing to and fro, I found myself beginning to nod off until I was startlingly jerked awake by a sudden braking of the car.

Had we hit something? No, it wasn't that. Peering through the gloom of the rain spattered windows, I could see what had happened. There on the road just in front of us, some 200 yards off, an elderly gentleman had come off his pushbike. Luke, to avoid hitting him and eager to assist, had performed an emergency stop.

The poor man had briefly lost consciousness, was very confused and in a lot of pain. He said he couldn't see properly then tried to stand up but immediately fell back onto his shoulder. He appeared to be suffering from mild concussion. After assessing his condition, we decided to call an ambulance. Alerting the security guard of the Sharpness dock, we assisted him in diverting the flow of traffic away from the area until the ambulance arrived. It took ages. Luke and Kevin heroically stood protectively over the gentleman, holding umbrellas to shield him from the worst of the weather and chatted to him to keep him alert.

One of the cars being diverted stopped behind us and four elderly gentlemen emerged from the vehicle. They had recognised the unfortunate man at once. He was part of their group of retired merchant navy sailors, and they had all been meeting up for a reunion that afternoon as Sharpness was where they had trained together so many years before. Touchingly, despite the trauma of the situation, they all pushed cash into our hands for the Teenage Cancer Trust charity when they learned what we were doing. One of the gentlemen told us, quite matter of factly, that he himself was terminally ill and that this would be the last reunion he would attend. Directly looking me in the eyes, he reminded me that life is short and that we should look out for each other and make every single day count. It made quite an impact on me.

Later that evening, sitting in the relative comfort of Kevin's caravan, we reflected on the events of the day. It had been quite eventful.

That night I chose to sleep alone in the tent (which Luke had kindly erected during the day) while Allan bunked down with the guys in the caravan. I valued that precious alone time. It gave me time to think. As I lay there, listening to the gentle pitter pattering of rain on the outside of the tent, snuggling comfortably into the warmth of the soft downy sleeping bag, I thought about how nice it had been to spend time walking with other people that day and I think it was at this point, with the prospect of various other friends meeting up with us from now on, that the realisation finally dawned on me. We were actually going to do it. We **would** finish the John O' Groats to Lands' End walk. I was sure of it.

Chapter 13 – Turning the Corner

Day Forty-Nine:

With renewed confidence and a sense of determination, we set off the following day towards the city of Bristol. Luke had been so kind to us, rising early himself to cook bacon and eggs especially for us to help us on our way that day. Once the soggy tent was packed away, he drove us back to Sharpness where we once again picked up the trail. The weather was overcast and cool but at least it wasn't raining!

For the first part of the day, we found ourselves walking along quiet country roads through some lovely villages and attractive market towns such as Berkeley. After some time, we joined the busy A38 and followed the adjoining footpath into Thornbury. By this time, it was late morning and we decided to stop for a drink in a pub we were passing. I am so glad we did.

Inside the pub, the landlord (a rather gruff looking fellow) asked us what we were doing with those heavy rucksacks. I thought he was going to chuck us out but as we told him, his whole demeanour changed. It turns out that he himself had once been an adventurer like us and had enjoyed hiking various long-distance trails. He lavished us with free drinks and made a very generous cash donation to the charity.

The young lad serving behind the bar was intrigued by our story and told us that he'd been invited by a mate to accompany him on one of the great American long-distance hiking routes but had so far declined. He was lacking confidence and didn't know if he wanted to put himself through the inconvenience of it, especially as he was worried that he might be tempted to give up halfway through. He was frightened of failure and of letting his friend down. But having heard us talking to the landlord, he felt inspired to at least pursue the possibility of accepting his friend's offer. "If you two can walk all that way, maybe I can too. After all, life's for living, isn't it?"

Leaving Thornbury, we re-joined the A38 and were rewarded by magnificent views: the vast expanse of water known as the Bristol Channel, the blue hills of Wales towering beyond and the majestic Severn Bridge, with its gleaming white pillars, linking England with Wales. We walked up and over Almond Hill, stopping to take photos at every opportunity, before crossing over both the M5 and the M4 motorways.

Picking our way through the Aztec Business Park on the outskirts of Bristol was challenging and we did get a bit lost but eventually we worked out where we should be. We had arranged to stay for the next couple of nights in the house of a lovely newlywed couple, Tim and Rebecca, who were closely related to good friends of ours. We were both looking forward to sleeping in a bed again and not having to walk with packs. As they knew they would both be out when we arrived, they had arranged for us to collect the key from a neighbour of theirs. Grateful to arrive, we took off our packs, left them in the front garden and went off to get the key.

We knocked on the neighbour's door. No reply. We rang the doorbell, repeatedly. Again, no reply. The neighbour was out! Uh oh. There was nothing else for it – we would just have to sit on our packs in the front garden and wait for Tim and Rebecca to get home, which wouldn't be for another three hours. As we sat there bemoaning our fate, a friendly voice called over from the house opposite. "Hello? ... Is everything alright? ... Can I help at all?"

We looked up to see a dark-haired woman in her late thirties, with sparkling eyes and a kindly disposition peering at us over the hedge. As soon as we'd explained to her our predicament, she warmly invited us to come over to her house for a cup of tea while we waited. She didn't know Tim and Rebecca at all as they'd only moved in recently but immediately welcomed us into her home, even though we were complete strangers to her.

Her house was a myriad of colours and textures. She was an artist and there were partially finished art projects everywhere we looked. It was homely and comforting. We enjoyed chatting over a cuppa for an hour or so before the neighbour with the key finally arrived home and we were able to collect it. When Tim and Rebecca arrived home that evening, they were amused to hear about our rendezvous with one of their neighbours. There it was once again – the kindness of strangers towards us. Tim and Rebecca were also lovely to us. They let us use their washing machine, fed us and were very hospitable. It was nice spending time getting to know them better.

Day Fifty:

The next morning dawned bright and clear. We walked the three miles from Patchway (where Tim and Rebecca lived) towards the heart of the city of Bristol. It felt good to walk without the burden of the rucksacks, weighing us down. Stopping for a comfort break in a small café on the Southmead Road, we were joined by our friend from home, Karen. It was the same Karen who had previously met up with us on our day off in Worcester, a week ago, but this time she was accompanied by her husband Andrew and today they had arranged to walk with us through the city.

It was great having companionship while we walked, and we really enjoyed chatting as we passed through the city. We soon crossed the common to the observatory, where we enjoyed wonderful views of the historic Clifton Suspension Bridge. The bridge, an iconic feat of Victorian engineering, spans a deep, urban river gorge. Isambard Kingdom Brunel's bridge stands proudly, linking the Clifton area of Bristol with the county of Somerset. It is an absolute masterpiece of industrial design.

Crossing over the bridge, we walked through Ashton Court Estate, a famous deer park, where we stopped to picnic on the wonderful provisions brought along by our friends. What a treat to have fresh fruit, yogurts, and all manner of other delights that we hadn't been able to enjoy for weeks and weeks due to their perishability and lack of portability. We had no access to a fridge while hiking! I can tell you, forced deprivation makes things taste all the better when you do finally get to enjoy them, and we were just so appreciative of that lunch.

At the end of the day, we had a brief spell of walking along the busy A38, which was tricky as there was no path but just a very overgrown grass verge. Before too long, we arrived at the airport, which was to be our finishing point for the day. We were driven back to Tim and Rebecca's house to spend one last night with them. Once again, we filled up Karen's car with 'stuff' we no longer needed to carry for her to take back home (Yes, Allan was still buying second hand books and CDs in charity shops we walked past). Saying goodbye to Karen and Andrew was strange as we knew that the next time we would see them, we would have finished the walk and be back at home again (and Allan would finally be reunited with all his precious purchases!).

***

Day Fifty-One:

We were fortunate enough the next morning to have Tim give us a lift back to yesterday's finishing point, although fitting three adults and two massive rucksacks into his mini was an interesting challenge with which to start the day. Finding ourselves walking along quiet country roads, we enjoyed lovely views of the gentle countryside surrounding us. At one point, we passed beside a large vineyard, where the grapes hung enticingly, waiting to be plucked. Picking our way carefully through a rather overgrown pathway, we were astonished to bump into a man who himself was walking from Lands' End to John O' Groats. Comparing notes was interesting and having picked his brain for tips for the next stage of our walk, we continued on our way.

After some time, we were fortunate enough to come across a picnic bench overlooking a lake, so we stopped for a bit to admire the view. It was a peaceful and isolated spot. Mother Nature had come into her own here – there were birds singing to each other in the trees surrounding us, butterflies fluttering from bush to bush, wildflowers and tall swaying grasses creating a magnificent display, grasshoppers and crickets chirping in the background. This was, I realised, one of those moments to savour.

It occurred to me again just how important it was to live in the moment and be fully present. Getting in touch with your senses and appreciating what is around you at any given moment in time. That was the true secret of happiness. I vowed to keep that truth, even in the midst of ordinary life back home. Only time would tell if I would be able to carry these lessons forward with me.

Eventually, we re-joined the road and followed it to a pretty village, where we stopped to eat our picnic lunch. Suitably fortified afterwards, we set out to face the challenge of the Mendips.

The Mendips are beautiful. They are an officially recognised AONB (Area of Outstanding Natural Beauty) and for good reason. This limestone range of hills stretches from the Bristol Channel in the West to the town of Frome, Somerset in the East. Walking up to the top of Black Down, the very highest point of the Mendips was challenging for sure, especially wearing fully laden rucksacks, but so worthwhile. Seemingly endless heather and bracken covered moorland stretched out in every direction.

As we stood on the site of the Bronze age barrows at the summit, a sense of awe came over us. Mankind from ancient times right up to the present day had stood in this very spot where we stood and doubtless future generations would too. It was humbling to realise our small place in the sweep of time.

I was delighted to discover wild Exmoor ponies roaming free among the rocky outcrops and trees. Under a small copse of trees, we came across some geometric grey concrete structures, half-hidden under vines and weeds. On closer inspection, we discovered what looked like the remains of some sort of military camp. We later discovered that all this crumbling masonry was in fact part of a bombing decoy town, designed to lure the German bombers of World War 2 into dropping their deadly loads over the unpopulated Mendips rather than the heavily populated city of Bristol. Ingenious idea!

Although we could have stayed up there on Black Down in the heart of the Mendips for hours and hours, eventually we decided it was time to move on. It was only four more miles to Cheddar Gorge, where we were booked into the hostel that night and it was all downhill from here, wasn't it? But not for the first time, we found ourselves lulled into a false sense of security.

The way down started off easily enough, following a farm track between the fields but soon the track petered out, leaving us initially with a waymarked footpath to follow. That should have been easy enough but as we progressed, the way got more and more challenging. This time our difficulties weren't caused by the overgrown vegetation but by loose rocks and slippery mud underfoot, which combined with increasingly steep slopes was treacherous.

Eventually we gave up on the official path and decided to follow a perimeter fence around the side of a quarry. This turned out to be a bad decision. It was horrible. We found ourselves slipping, sliding, and clambering down steep inclines, having to negotiate narrow spaces between trees with our rucksacks and grabbing hold of whatever we could to steady ourselves (tree roots, fences, branches). We scrambled along making slow progress.

Allan took a tumble not once but twice. Fortunately, he wasn't badly hurt on either occasion. I was petrified of falling catastrophically, as I had the previous year, and breaking more limbs. But somehow, we made it down. It felt quite surreal emerging from this nightmare straight into the heart of a housing estate on the outskirts of Cheddar Gorge. Seeking refuge in a pub, we waited for the adrenaline surge to subside, so we could breathe again, before taking a look around Cheddar Gorge.

The town of Cheddar Gorge was another tourist hotspot. Filled with holidaymakers buzzing around the eateries and gift shops like bees, this town was not what I had expected at all. It was pretty enough – steep cliffs (home to a colony of feral goats apparently) overlooking the quaint riverside town with its waterfall, craft shops and cafes but it was absolutely cram-packed with tourists. Not only that but most of the official attractions were shut due to a COVID-19 outbreak in the local area.

In contrast, the hostel was lovely – modern, clean, and spacious with excellent facilities. We were thankful to arrive after what had turned out to be quite a hard day.

Day Fifty-Two:

I started the day by chatting to an American woman staying in the hostel with her young family. I discovered that she was from Santa Cruz in California, a place that held fond memories for me, as my very good friend Melanie lives there. After the friendly chat over breakfast, we set off at about 8am and enjoyed walking along deserted country roads. In contrast to the hilly terrain we'd tackled the previous day, this area was completely flat. There would be no inclines to face at all.

 Stretching out before us, we could see mile upon mile of flat agricultural land, broken only by the hedgerows and trees lining the edges of the fields. Distances were quite deceptive here. Glastonbury Tor stood out as a beacon among the vast featureless landscape and behind us the Mendips served as a reminder to be grateful for an easier walk that day.

Walking through a small but very picturesque village, we were stopped by a gentleman trimming his hedge, who was curious as to why we were walking through the village with such heavy packs. He invited us into his garden for a cup of tea as he wanted to talk further and find out a bit more about our adventure. Happy to oblige, we enjoyed a very pleasant half-hour drinking tea and chatting to the couple, who were recently retired teachers. I hope in some way we may have inspired them to take on an adventure of their own.

A bit further along, we came across another couple of long-distance hikers, which was obvious from their heavy packs. Unlike us, they were young and fit. Much younger than us. We found out that they were also walking from John O' Groats to Lands' End but that they had taken a different route from us and had started two weeks before us. They were expecting to walk for another three weeks before finishing as they would soon be joining the South-West Coast path to end their route. We were taking a much more direct route and only had twelve days of walking left now. It was interesting comparing notes. They were also raising money for the same charity as us – The Teenage Cancer Trust. What a coincidence! We said our goodbyes and wished them well with the rest of their trip.

Gradually the farming land gave way to vast grassy marshland, interspersed with water-filled ditches. The Somerset Levels are one of the largest remaining wetlands left in England and have great ecological significance, providing a uniquely suitable habitat for many species of insects, birds, and flora. It boasts of hosting the largest lowland population of breeding wading birds, such as lapwings, snipe, curlew and redshanks, in the whole of southern England; it was a bird watcher's paradise.

Although it was flat, for which we were grateful, it was also a monotonous and tedious landscape through which to walk. This, coupled with the fact that we still ached from the strenuous nature of the previous day's walk, made it a long, hard day. By the end of it, we were sore and tired. Grateful to finally arrive at the campsite, which strangely seemed to be in someone's back garden on the outskirts of Bridgewater, we put up the tent, helped along by the free-range chickens running around the site, all of which seemed intrigued by what we were doing and eager to assist!

Day Fifty-Three:

The following morning, after packing up camp, we set off along the Bridgewater and Taunton Canal. It was a lovely route with well-maintained towpaths and made all the more interesting by the 'Somerset Space Walk' – a series of scale models of the planets of our solar system, spaced out at regular intervals along a fourteen-mile stretch of the canal tow path.

At one point, we came across a man sitting on top of a small barge with some kind of machinery attached, which was chugging its way slowly up the canal. This was apparently a dredging barge as the canal was being cleaned. We saw several other people who were working on the overgrown banks. They were all regular volunteers and were engaged in valuable conservation work. We got chatting to them about their work and they generously gave us a cash donation for the charity, along with instructions to stop for coffee at a highly recommended canal side café just a bit further along.

After lunch, we walked as far as Creech St Michael, where we came off the canal towpath. Passing a small Baptist church, we were delighted to see a sign advertising coffee and homemade cake. Speeding up, we jauntily made our way to the church car park where a tent had been set up along with tables and chairs.

"Coffee and cake please."

"Sorry love, we've just closed for the day." The man behind the table must have noticed our disappointed expressions.

"Just a minute….." He disappeared into the church building, only to re-emerge a few minutes later bearing two steaming hot mugs of coffee and a plate with two large slices of delicious home-made chocolate cake. "There's no charge for these, we're all very interested in what you two are up to and why you are carrying those enormous rucksacks."

Encouraged by his words and re-energised by the cake, we told him our story. Soon we had quite a gathering of church folks around us. They were all friendly and kindly told us of a better route we could take, off road, alongside the river. We took their advice and enjoyed a lovely walk through the countryside, following the riverside path to the village of Ruiston, where we decided to stop and dry out our tent in the park before making our way to the Holiday Inn where we were booked for the night. It didn't take long to dry the soggy tent and we figured that it was an awful lot easier to dry it in the sun than trying to dry it out by spreading it all over the hotel room that evening.

Once everything was dry and packed neatly away once again, we continued on to the hotel, where my brother and my dad were waiting to take us out for a meal that evening. It was a lovely way to end the day. It was great catching up with the family news and they kept reiterating just how proud they all were of us.

At one point during the evening, my brother turned to me, looked me in the eyes.

"Tell me Debbie, what's it really like?" he asked earnestly, "I imagine it's been simply amazing doing this walk?" I think he was having some kind of mid-life crisis and the thought of leaving all his responsibilities behind and walking into the sunset appealed to him. I thought carefully for a minute about how to answer the question.

"Well, to tell you the truth, most of it has been a slog, we've just been trudging along for mile after mile after mile each and every day. Yes, there have been some amazing times but most of the time it's just been the two of us trundling endlessly

along." I could see the disappointment in his eyes. It was true....
most of the time we just kept putting one foot in front of
the other, whether we felt like it or not, covering the distance
incrementally each day, making slow but steady progress. That's
another one of those lessons – things I learned along the way:
great things are achieved through lots of tiny steps and those
seemingly insignificant steps add up. At the end of the day, we
had kept going through sheer hard work and determination.

After the meal, we said our goodbyes to dad and Jon, knowing
that it wouldn't be too long before we saw them again, by which
time we'd have finished the walk. We now had just over a week
left before we reached Lands' End.

At the hotel, our good friend Jill Jennings was waiting for us,
along with her daughter Lydia. They had driven over to Devon
to join us for a few days and would not only be supporting us as
we walked but also staying in the same hotels as us for the next
couple of nights. It was great to see them and a relief to know
that once again we wouldn't have to carry our packs for a few
days – they would be our 'baggage transfer' service.

Jill, a kind-hearted, caring person, and a nurse by trade, asked
us how we were doing physically. Allan reported that his feet
were still causing him issues due to the infection from the
burst blister he'd suffered many weeks ago in Scotland. She
immediately asked to see his feet, then cleaned and re-dressed
the wounds for him. She was so matter of fact about it that he
didn't have time to be embarrassed and we spent the rest of the
evening laughing and chatting. Good friends are a special gift. I
was looking forward to the next few days.

There was another rather special way in which Jill was able to
assist us too. Allan's walking boots, which he had purchased
cheaply in Fort William many weeks ago, had broken: one of the
soles had parted company with the boot. Whilst we walked the
following day (with Allan wearing trainers), she took the boots
to a cobbler and got them repaired for him. The cobbler made no

charge for this when he found out what they were being used for. Those may have been made for walking but maybe not quite so far! We'd tested them to their limits that's for sure. At least we could continue on knowing that we both had stout footwear with which to finish the trip.

Chapter 14 – From Cream Teas to Pasties

Day Fifty-Four:

Leaving our packs with Jill, who kindly supplied us with snacks to keep us going throughout the day, we made our way through the town of Taunton, with its very ugly and out of place looking council office building. Leaving Taunton behind, we passed through a series of beautiful villages before turning off down a small country lane. Today's route was so quiet and peaceful. We didn't even mind having to climb up a steep hill, especially as the views from the top were amazing. We enjoyed ambling along, chatting to a few people we encountered here and there. It was very relaxing. After ten miles or so, we were met by Jill and Lydia, and we found a quiet churchyard in which to stop for a picnic lunch. It was a perfect spot with extensive views over the Blackdown Hills.

After lunch, we passed from Somerset into the county of Devon where the small country lanes underwent a dramatic change. Instead of level roads, edged with grass verges, we were faced with steep-sided sunken lanes edged with red mud banks. Fortunately for us the roads were quiet and pretty much deserted but when the odd car passed by it was tricky trying to get out of the way! When we got to the village of Culmstock, we came across the Culm Valley Inn – a great place to stop for a drink. From there, we followed the riverside path for the remaining three miles into Uffculme.

Here we once again met up with Jill and Lydia and made our way to the village pub where we were booked to stay for the night. Opening the door of the pub, we were met with suspicious looks as a dozen pairs of eyes fixed us to the spot. It seemed that the locals weren't too used to strangers in these parts and looked at us as if we'd come from another planet. It didn't seem particularly friendly. What's more, the pub itself didn't serve food and we were very hungry by that time. In the end, we resorted to a takeaway meal which we ate in the pub 'garden' – not so much a garden as a stepped terrace of paving slabs beyond the car park.

An old work colleague of mine, Jaki, had moved to the local area and drove over to see us that evening. Sitting on the terrace, she told us all about the ways of the Devonshire locals and she even took our dirty washing back to her house to wash, with the promise of returning it the following evening to our next stopping point.

Day Fifty-Five:

The next day started out with us walking once again along quiet country lanes, passing through the strangely named village of Britham Bottom, then through Butterleigh, before arriving at the village of Bickleigh around lunchtime. Why do all the Devonshire villages seem to start with the letter B? It was a pleasant enough walk that morning.

In Bickleigh we discovered a gem of a place – a mill side craft shop and café, with a small museum attached. Here we stopped to experience our first taste of proper Devonshire scones. Cream before jam or jam before cream? That was the question we asked ourselves before indulging, knowing that to get the order wrong could cause great offence to the locals. A quick internet search enlightened us – ah... here in Devon it was definitely cream before jam, whilst in Cornwall it was the other way round. Suitably fortified, we continued on our way.

The road we needed to follow to travel from Bickleigh to Crediton was the A3072. It was not such a pleasant road to walk along. It was steeply hilly, had many twists and turns, was extremely busy with holiday traffic and unfortunately there was no footpath. We were back to traffic dodging again but this time the drivers were racing along as if this was a motorway – all in a desperate hurry to get to their destinations. As well as all this, it was unpleasantly hot that day and even though we didn't have to carry our rucksacks as Jill was transporting them for us, we found ourselves struggling. After Allan narrowly escaped being hit by a car, we stuck more closely together and picked our way quite slowly and carefully along the road. We really didn't know how much further we could keep going and were just about ready to give up, when we came across something that lifted our spirits.

As we rounded yet another corner after one particularly steep climb, we saw an unexpected sight – peculiarly, there straight ahead of us was a roadside ice-cream hut, with a bench beside it. An ice-cream hut in the middle of nowhere? How strange. As no-one was around, we put some money in the honesty box and helped ourselves to one of the deliciously cold, sweet treats. Sitting on the bench outside, we contemplated whether to phone Jill and ask her to rescue us but reasoned that as it was only another three miles before we finished, we would somehow manage to see it through.

Surprisingly, the next three miles proved to be much better than we anticipated (possibly aided by the energy burst that the ice cream had given us). The views over the Devonshire countryside were lovely, the road levelled and straightened out and before long there was a path to walk on, which made our walk much safer.

Walking into Crediton, we found it to be a very pleasant place. Apart from a brief interlude, walking across a rugby ground and having to the retrace our steps as there was no exit the other side, we found the hotel without too much trouble. At the hotel, Jill and Lydia were once again waiting for us. Enjoying our final evening together, we were delighted when Jaki and her husband drove over and joined us for a drink. Not only had she brought our clean washing as promised, but also offered to take our camping stuff and deliver it to the campsite we would stay in on Tuesday night. Such kindness was touching, and we were very grateful. We felt truly spoiled. Everyone was going out of their way to help us reach that finish line.

Day Fifty-Six:

The next day was no different – the encouragement of friends continued in the form of our old friends Nel and Richard. Having said farewell to Jill and Lydia and thanking them profusely for the amazing support they'd given us, we were greeted by Nel and Richard who had spent the night sleeping in their campervan in order to join us for the day. The plan was that Nel would walk the whole route that day with us whilst Richard supported us in the van.

Nel. She is one of a kind. An extraordinary person that I feel privileged to be able to call a friend of mine. I will never forget the day we first met each other. I was eighteen years old, away from home for the first time, shy and incredibly lacking in self-confidence. She was dazzling – long, red hair, incredibly sporty and she exuded confidence. I'd never seen anyone quite like her before. She was dazzling and would just light up any room she entered. Amazingly, we found ourselves sharing a room together in our first year at college and we became close friends even though we were very different from each other. We were such an incongruous pair. I was incredibly insecure, mediocre at everything and very introverted, whereas she was an extrovert, and a popular, high achiever. She may be very different from me, but she was and still is one of the kindest and most genuine people I know.

It was a good walk that day and time just flew by. The route was varied and gave Nel a taste of everything – we walked along quiet country lanes, across fields, following signposted footpaths and then a short stretch right at the end of the day walking alongside a busy road in the pouring rain. It was lovely to have company and we had plenty of opportunities to catch up on the last few years of each other's lives as we walked.

The encouragement of coming across the iconic red campervan at various points in the day just added to the delight. Before we knew it, we'd arrived in Okehampton, our finishing point for the day. Saying goodbye, we promised to keep in touch and meet up again soon. Nel had done well to walk the eighteen miles that day without building up to it and I hoped that she didn't suffer too much the following day. It's relatively easy walking those distances when you've trained for it and have been regularly doing so for a couple of months but for someone not used to it, it could be challenging and uncomfortable afterwards.

Lying in bed that night, I reflected, with a sense of contentment, on the day we'd just had. We were truly blessed to have so many good friends and such a supportive family. Together, they were virtually carrying us through this final stretch. In less than one week from now we would be back home, and it would all be over. Just a few more days to go.

***

Day Fifty-Seven:

Our final Monday of walking dawned bright and fair. Having said goodbye to our friends yesterday, we were once again on our own today, and carrying our packs once more (although greatly helped by the fact that Jaki still had our camping equipment, thus making our loads somewhat lighter). We began by making the stiff climb out of Okehampton to join the Granite Way, an off-road cycle track, stretching for eleven miles through the beautiful Devonshire countryside.

The Granite Way was a delight from start to finish. Tree-lined paths following the route of an old disused railway line made for easy walking: flat, level and straight. The views over the Devonshire countryside and Dartmoor beyond were spectacular. Not only were we afforded magnificent scenery, but the route was interesting. It was full of industrial heritage. The Granite Way follows the route of the old Southern Region railway line, built to transport goods and visitors from London to Plymouth in the west country.

At one point we passed an old railway carriage graveyard. It was surreal seeing the old rusty hulks of these massive beasts just standing there, seemingly loitering around without point or purpose. I wondered what stories they could tell of times of old. Of passengers and loads they'd once carried. Of important work they'd been involved in. Of untold mysteries and secrets they'd held. They weren't about to give up their stories easily. Leaving the eerie scrapyard behind, we continued on.

Before long we found ourselves crossing the famous Meldon Viaduct. Built in 1874, the viaduct spans 165 metres in length, over the remains of several disused mineral mines. Looking down was disconcerting for anyone scared of heights (I count myself one of them!). The trees and features below us looked miniscule; at this point we were one hundred and fifty-one feet above the valley below. From the mid-point of the viaduct, we could see as far as the dam at Meldon and a large reservoir to the south. It was impressive and I wondered how the Victorians had managed such a feat of engineering without all our modern technology and state of the art equipment.

Arriving in Lydford, with its spectacular waterfall lined gorge, we stopped for a drink in the village pub. A gentleman came over to chat to us – he was a fellow hiker and had recognised by the 'look' of us that we were too (the packs were a bit of a clue!). He was just taking a bit of time out of his busy work schedule to hike around Dartmoor alone and told us about some of the longer adventures he'd had in the past. He made a generous donation to the charity before heading off himself. Setting off again, we made our way along the road towards Tavistock.

As we walked along the small B-road, the countryside around us began to open up. Instead of the densely tree-lined verges we'd become used to, we were treated to increasingly tantalising views of the beautiful open Devonshire farmscape, with its rich red soil. Beyond us, in the distance we could see a lone hill rising up with some sort of ruin atop. As we got closer, the stunning St Michaels church became clearer. Perched high up on Brent Tor, this twelfth century chapel is one of West Devon's most iconic landmarks. It claims to be the highest working church in England and is a stunningly beautiful setting, ideal for a wedding. It's no wonder that so many are held here over the summer months.

We decided to take the brief detour to explore further and spent a happy half-hour or so just rambling around the hilltop church, enjoying the views from our elevated position. Allan did a quick sketch while I indulged in a spot of smartphone photography. Arriving sometime later in Tavistock, we found the hotel and gratefully collapsed into the comfy beds. Tomorrow we would once again be under canvas.

***

Day Fifty-Eight:

The following day, we started out early, walking along quiet country roads once more. Before long we reached a very important checkpoint: the River Tamar. Crossing over the Tamar Bridge, we left Devon behind and entered the Duchy of Cornwall, our final county of the trip. It was an emotional moment for both of us. One of the locals noticed us and having chatted with us, she left us with her best wishes for a successful end to the trip and a generous cash donation for the charity. Climbing up a steep hill, we left Tamar Bridge behind and walked to the small village of Kelly Brae, where we had lunch in the pub.

It was the sound that hit us first – a distant but steadily growing rumble, reminiscent of thunder, although the sky was clear and bright. As we progressed along the road, the roar grew louder, building up to some sort of crescendo. We were perplexed. What on Earth could it be? Rounding a corner, we were faced with a deafening blast, and we finally discovered the source of the strange sounds we'd been hearing out here in the deserted Cornish countryside.

Tall factory buildings stood beside the road, perched somewhat precariously on the steep cliff sides of an enormous working quarry. Gigantic conveyor belts transporting hunks of granite trundled along above our heads. The impressive, if somewhat jarring sound of industrial machinery performing its daily tasks screamed out at us, demanding our attention. Although it was fascinating to get this glimpse into a working quarry, we hurried quickly through, desperate to escape the tumultuous din.

Before too long, we once again found ourselves walking along deserted country roads. Peace was restored. As we passed through one village after another, we began to see signs of the rich industrial heritage of the area. The ruins of disused shafts and engine houses, remnants of a once thriving tin mining industry, littered the countryside around us. Obviously, this area hadn't always been so peaceful, but was once a hive of activity.

In the 19th century, Cornwall was one of the richest mining areas in the world, driven predominantly by the extraction of tin and copper. And today there is some discussion around the possibility of reopening the mines, as the area has been found to be rich in lithium, essential for both our portable electronics and for the batteries of electric vehicles. We stopped briefly to look around the ruins of a mining settlement in Pensilva, before continuing on to the campsite where we were booked for the night.

The campsite was delightful. We were warmly greeted by Catherine, the most hospitable campsite owner we'd ever had the privilege to meet. Welcoming us to the site, she quickly provided tea and home-made cake, along with chairs (so we didn't have to sit on the floor) not only to us but for our good friend Jaki as well, who had gone out of her way to bring us our camping equipment for the night, so we didn't have to carry it over the past few days. The campsite owner showed us round the excellent facilities, before promising she would return in the morning with porridge and tea for us to enjoy before we left!

Day Fifty-Nine:

True to her word, early the following day we were treated to porridge, Cornish style, with strawberries and clotted cream on top along with steaming mugs of hot tea and a generous cash donation for the charity. She would take no money for her kind service. It was an amazing start to the day.

As we'd planned a twenty-three-mile route that day, we knew we were in for a particularly tough day. It was made even harder by the fact that, after three days of walking light, we were once again carrying fully laden rucksacks. By this point in the trip though, we knew we were on the home straight. In just a few days it would all be over. This gave us the strength we needed to get through the day. Well, that fact coupled with the fact that we were fuelled up by the calorie-dense breakfast at the start of the day! By eight O' clock, we were packed up and raring to go.

There were lots of hills today – the quiet country lanes seemed to undulate; one minute we were climbing up a steep slope, the next descending into a valley. This went on and on. At one point we passed a friendly couple of mature ladies. They were friends and were making their way into the village of St Neots for a social gathering of some sort. They got chatting to us and invited us to come along to their coffee morning.

Well, you can't ignore an offer like that can you? So, we accompanied them to the village hall. What a welcome awaited us! This was the first time since lockdown that the 'Old Codgers' group had been able to meet in person and their absolute joy in being able to do so was infectious. The room was packed with mature folk. Everyone there may have been over the age of sixty-five, but they sure knew how to have a good time. Chatting together over biscuits, coffee and cake, laughter spilled out of them. Their joy was infectious.

They were intrigued by our journey and treated us like visiting celebrities. At one point they decided to have a whip round and collected cash and notes to present to us for the charity. They were some of the nicest people we'd had the privilege of meeting on our entire trip. I was struck by the pleasure they took in simple everyday things. Instead of focussing on and moaning about their various aches and pains (and judging by the number of walking frames littered around the room there must have been plenty), they delighted in the simple joy of being in each other's company. I still find myself smiling when I think of that Old Codgers group, on the edge of Bodmin Moor. I'd say, that it was definitely one of the highlights of the trip.

Finally tearing ourselves away from the lovely folk we'd met, we continued on our way across Bodmin Moor to the National Trust property of Lanhydrock. It was mobbed! So many people all visiting on the same day. We had planned to stop here for lunch, but the queues were ridiculously long, stretching round the front of the estate and into the car park. In the end, we just sat down for a bit and gave up on the idea of proper lunch. Instead, we made do with what we had with us.

Even this proved challenging as the number of wasps all hovering around in the hope of some tasty morsel made it difficult to relax. Whilst we might ordinarily have spent some time looking around, we decided that it was far too busy, so after a short break we headed off again. We'd come back to Lanhydrock another time, when it was less busy.

The rest of the day was just a long slog, trudging tediously through the country lanes for mile after mile until eventually arriving at the pop-up eco campsite we'd booked for the night. This was basically a farmer's field with a compost toilet and a solitary tap with some running cold water. Not quite the luxury we'd enjoyed at the previous night's campsite. But by the time we arrived, we were both too tired to care and sunk gratefully into our sleeping bags, exhausted from the long day we'd just had.

Just four days left and none of them as long as today's walk. It should be easier from now on.

Chapter 15 - The Final Stretch

Day Sixty:

We awoke the next morning to steady drizzle or 'mizzle' as the locals call it. The farmers field which was being used as the 'eco' campsite was a quagmire. Mud was everywhere. Ugh. I was glad we weren't camping here with young children as I can't imagine it would be much fun in the rain. Packing up our soggy, mud-covered tent, we set off once again.

The day started badly. Looking over the route for the day, we'd decided to follow a marked footpath rather than the more straightforward road route so that we could avoid the traffic.

At first the footpath was ok but before long it became more and more overgrown, until we reached a point at which it was completely impassable. Although we'd only walked a few miles by then, it was frustrating having to retrace our route back to the road, which we then followed, careful to avoid passing traffic and very aware of reduced visibility due to the adverse weather conditions, even though we were wearing high visibility coats and using the high vis rain covers for our packs.

Passing through St Austell, we found a coffee shop and decided to stop for bacon butties and coffee. During the time it took us to eat the breakfast, the rain increased and by the time we were ready to leave, instead of a constant drizzle it was raining heavily. The thought of continuing did not fill us with joy, but what was the alternative? Resigned to our fate, we once again put on our packs and stepped outside to continue walking through the steady rain.

After following the roads out of the town, we were dismayed to see that the footpath ran out. There was nothing for it – we were back dodging traffic on the edge of a fast A road again. This time however there was the added stress of knowing there was such poor visibility for the car drivers. It was a very stressful part of the walk. Hurriedly, we got off the road as soon as we possibly could. We judged that it was better to add a few extra miles if we needed to for the sake of safety. Better to arrive alive than be killed on the way!

We found ourselves walking through endless country lanes with no sign of shop or pub or even a bench on which to sit for a while. After sixteen miles of this, we were both extremely fed up and grumpy with each other. No doubt, part of this was due to the aftereffects of our twenty-three mile hike the previous day.

Around 3pm we came across a settlement which had a pub and a small post office selling coffee, so we decided that this would be a good place to stop for a late lunch. Eagerly we went up to the pub door and gratefully turned the handle, desperate for some lunch and a rest. It was locked. There was no one around. Oh well, we could always get some coffee and food in the small post office shop across the road.... But it too was closed. Ugh. We searched our packs for what food we could find – only hiking snacks left. So that day, our late lunch consisted of jelly babies and crisps. Very healthy!

Our spirits lifted somewhat at the end of the day when Martin, our 'trail angel' whom we had met in Sutherland, picked us up and whisked us off to stay at his house for the night. Cathy and Martin were incredibly hospitable and made us feel right at home straight away. After the exhausting and difficult day we'd had trudging through the rain, it was so nice to be treated to a hot cooked meal, warm showers, and a comfortable bed. Their house was lovely and we enjoyed stunning views over the Cornish countryside from our bedroom window. They even had a gorgeous golden retriever puppy called Bear, who was quite cute! They spoilt us, which was great as today was definitely a low point.

Day Sixty-One:

Having enjoyed a leisurely breakfast with Cathy and Martin the next morning, we set off once again. Cathy kindly made packed lunches for us to take with us and Martin delivered our rucksacks to the campsite for us, so that we didn't have to carry them that day. We are so grateful for their kindness. They definitely helped us reach the end.

We followed the small Cornish lanes to the village of Chacewater, then joined a busy A road to the hamlet of Todpool, where we managed to pick up a footpath which led us all the way to St Day. We stopped for lunch here, before setting off in the direction of Redruth and walking through the fascinating mining heritage sites. Taking this particular route was not only atmospheric but also educational and extremely interesting.

Instead of racing ahead in his usual manner, Allan slowed right down and today we walked together, side by side at a leisurely pace, chatting and savouring the time we had left on the walk, knowing that in just a few days it would all be over.

As we approached the campsite where we had booked to stay that night, we enjoyed our first tantalising sight of the sea... a reminder that we were so close now! It was our first glimpse of the sea for eight weeks and we felt a surge of excitement on seeing it again.

The Pioneer Billy campsite was great, and the owner Carol was really nice. She let us camp there for free as we were raising money for charity. Dinner was once again our staple fall-back meal of dehydrated cheesy mashed potato with sardines, which we ate resignedly, knowing that this could well be the very last time we ate it (hopefully!). That evening, looking over the following day's sixteen-mile route and the expected wet and miserable weather conditions, I resolved to enjoy the final two days no matter what came our way.

Day Sixty-Two:

The next day felt long and tiring. It seemed to go on for ever. Maybe it was exacerbated by the knowledge that we were so very close to the finish? I'm not sure but it was certainly a challenge even though we had definitely faced harder and more physically demanding days on our trip. We started out by trudging through the rain.

After about five miles of slogging along with our heavy packs, we decided to take them off and sit on them to catch our breath for a few minutes. Just as we sat down, a large lorry swept past us, sending a torrent of dirty rainwater from the road surface in our direction. The wall of muddy brown water hit us like a tsunami and in an instant, we were drenched. There was nothing for it but to continue walking the rest of the way into Hayle, where we stopped to dry out for a while, enjoying Cornish pasties and tea before setting out to cross from the north coast to the south coast. Thankfully, by the time we had almost reached the south coast, the rain had cleared away and had been replaced by bright sunshine and a fresh breeze.

We saw the iconic St Michael's Mount rising in front of us before we spotted the sea. This rocky island just off the coast of Marazion, crowned with an impressive medieval castle, is a magnet for visitors and no wonder. Managed by the National Trust, this extraordinary site is only accessible at low tide. Reaching the peak of the hilly footpath, we were stopped in our tracks by the beauty of the scene. Snowy-white topped waves crashed against the rocky, granite outcrops forming the coastline. An expanse of glistening sapphire stretched out before us, speckled with diamonds of intensely bright light. It was dazzling.

When we got to the beach, we spent some time taking it all in and enjoying the lovely weather for a bit. The windy conditions meant that although it was too rough for swimming, we were treated to the beauty of foamy white horses crashing on the shore. We took off our packs and just enjoyed sitting on the sandy beach for a while, soaking up the sunshine.

After regaining some strength, helped no doubt by the deliciously creamy Cornish ice cream we'd enjoyed at the beach, we decided to follow the South-West Coast Path towards Penzance. Unfortunately, we discovered that after about a mile or so, it had been blocked off for maintenance. Grr....so annoying! Once again, we found ourselves re-tracing our steps to then follow an alternative route alongside the road. Honestly, we must have added mile upon mile of unnecessary walking to our journey by having to re-trace our steps so many times during the course of the entire trip.

The campsite for our final night in Cornwall was not good. It was expensive and was basically just a pop-up campsite on a farmer's field. Although we had already booked and paid for a pitch for a two-man tent, the owners demanded extra money for the second person as soon as we arrived. There was no friendly welcome at this campsite! It just seemed to be all about profit. What's more, the pitch we were given was on a slope – that's not great if you are sleeping in a tent. But quite honestly, by the time we'd pitched the tent, we were just so exhausted that we no longer cared.

This day had certainly been a challenge, but we only had one day left now. "It's not over until it's over." Allan reminded me before we both fell into the deepest slumber of the trip.

That final night, I slept like a log. My smart watch informed me the next morning that of my nine hours total sleep time, I had enjoyed six whole hours of deep sleep during the night!

***

Day Sixty-Three:

The final day. Here we were, about to finish the journey. There was no longer any shadow of doubt in my mind that we would do it. By the end of today, we would officially be able to call ourselves 'End-to-Enders'. We would have walked the entire length of the United Kingdom, from the northernmost tip of Scotland to the most southerly point in England. And we'd have done it in nine weeks, rather than the customary twelve weeks that most people take. Not bad for a pair of unfit, middle aged non-walkers.

The last day was quite an emotional day for me. I think it was partly due to the realisation that I was about to conquer the momentous challenge that I'd set myself so many months beforehand. It was the fulfilment of a dream for me. All those months ago, I'd resolved to test my mettle and I can honestly say that throughout this journey, my mettle had well and truly been tested.

In part though, I felt an overwhelming sadness that it was all about to come to an end. There was a simplicity in this life. Just walking, eating and sleeping every single day. Over and over again. The routine was comforting. I thought glumly of the life back home that awaited me – stressful, overly busy, complicated. I wasn't looking forward to a return to that life.

But on the other hand, I was excited too: it would be wonderful to see my lovely boys again later today and it would be great to catch up with family and friends back home. A complete mixture of emotions flooded through me.

***

We woke early, packed up camp for the very last time, (as we did so, noticing that one of the guy ropes had finally given way but this little tent had done well to last as long as it had) and set off towards the centre of the town.

Penzance was delightful; narrow cobbled streets lined with quaint quirky houses and a famous haunt for pirates in times gone by. Leaving the centre of town, we strode confidently along the picturesque seafront before heading inland, climbing steeply for a mile or so. It was certainly an excellent early morning warm up! It struck me again that by now, we weren't at all intimidated by hills. We were used to them.

Leaving Penzance behind, we walked along the quiet lanes to the village of St Buryan, where we bought drinks and snacks before resting awhile on the picnic bench in the village. There was certainly no need to hurry today – we only had eleven miles to walk and plenty of time in which to walk it. Crossing over to Sennen Cove on the north coast, we stopped and enjoyed lunch on the picturesque beach. Leaving the rucksacks with me, Allan went for his final swim of the trip.

As I sat there alone in the glorious sunshine, I counted my blessings. I felt an incredible urge to freeze this moment in time. To not just momentarily suspend the movement of time but to stop it in its tracks. Well, obviously, I couldn't do that, so I did the next best thing: I savoured the present. What a day to end the journey; it was a truly halcyon day. I looked around at the scene before me with a sense of overwhelming gratitude.

The glorious deep-blue sea stretched out to the horizon like a mirror, shimmering with reflected sunlight. Above my head, islands of white floated lazily across the azure blue sky. Relaxing in the warm sunshine, listening to the whisper of waves as they met the salt strand, I inhaled deeply, enjoying the sweet aroma of salty sea air being diffused by the gentle breeze currently caressing my cheeks. Dark pools of infinity littered the shore, contrasting with the creamy, smooth softness of the sandy beach. A sudden movement caught my eye – the scuttling of a small crab to a nearby rock. This was it. This was paradise. It was right before me, right here on Earth. If only we have eyes to see the wonders around us.

***

The last three miles of walking along the South-West Coast Path from the beach at Sennen Cove to Land's End was idyllic. We were treated to spectacular cliff top views as we made our way through fields of brightly coloured wildflowers. Great flocks of seabirds called noisily to each other as they wheeled around us, whilst others nested precariously on the steep cliff sides. We took our time, drinking in all that nature had to offer. It felt as if this was our reward for persevering through the challenges, the struggles, and the lowest points of the trip: this was truly the icing on the cake. It was a wonderful way to finish the journey.

As we drew nearer to the collection of white buildings making up the Land's End Centre, our footsteps grew slower. Subconsciously, we were trying to delay our arrival, heralding the end of this great adventure. Despite this, eventually we arrived. Putting down our packs at the entrance gate, we grabbed an innocent bystander and implored him to take our photo, which he did. He seemed suitably impressed by our efforts.

After the impromptu 'photoshoot', we made our way to the hotel to have our papers stamped as proof we'd made it all the way from one end to the other. This would be an important piece of evidence if we decided to apply for the official certificate, certifying that we had earned the right to call ourselves 'End-to-Enders'. After spending some time looking around the free museum about famous End-to-End journeys, we sat down for a celebratory drink whilst we waited for our boys, Luke and Andrew. It felt rather strange knowing that we'd done it; it was almost an anti-climax. What now? What next?

"Mum!" Luke grinned as he hugged me warmly, "You did it! I'm so proud of you."

"Gosh, these bags are heavy.... how on Earth did you manage to carry them all that way?" asked Andrew, lugging them into the boot of Luke's car.

It was lovely to see these two strapping lads after so many weeks apart and we were so grateful they'd offered to collect us and drive us back home. It was surreal whizzing through place after place we'd taken days to walk through!

So that was it, the journey was over. But in some ways, it was just the beginning. I'd learned so much about myself, about other people, about the world around us. Incorporating the lessons I'd learned along the way would take a lifetime.

Journeying. The truth is that we are all on a journey. Not everyone has the chance to do what we did but all of us are travelling. From the moment we enter the world to the moment we depart; we are all on a journey through time. How we will choose to spend that time is up to us. Whether we rush through life, stressed, world weary and tired or choose instead to pause, to savour, to enjoy each moment and discover the wonder of the life that we've been gifted, is up to us.

Allan and I may physically have walked from one end of the country to another, but our journey was more than just a geographical one. Yes, it was physical, but it was also emotional, personal and spiritual. The sights we saw, the people we met, the experiences we had, all contributed to the journey we went on. We grew as people, we changed, we learned more about ourselves than ever before.

This journey shaped us. We will never be the same.

Chapter 16 – The Ending is Just the Beginning

The greatest gift this walk gave me was the gift of time. Time to pause, to step out of my busy life, to reflect and to ponder. It was cathartic and liberating. It taught me so much and it's the lessons I learned on the walk that will inform how I live out the remainder of my days.

These lessons can be summed up in three words:

Simplicity

Community

Gratitude

They are among the greatest truths I will take from this time.

Simplicity:

We all have a tendency to cram our diaries full of events and say "yes" to everything anyone asks of us. We over complicate things. Too many commitments, too much stuff. Not enough time. Our lives end up in a tangled out of control mess, which can cause us great stress. The answer is to simplify. What do you actually need? Ask this of your clothes, your furniture, the contents of all those cupboards cram packed and overflowing. All we needed for nine solid weeks was contained within one rucksack.

So why do we feel the need to gather and hoard? Learn to say "no" to demands on your time rather than acquiescing to every request. Give yourself time to think before committing to anything. Ask yourself whether this something that will add stress or will energise you. Are you acting out of a sense of duty or a desire to get involved? Are you looking for the approval and affirmation of other people? Do you have a fear of missing out? These are important questions to consider. Keep it simple whenever you can.

Community:

'No man is an island' declared John Donne and he was right. We are social beings, and we need each other. Develop friendships. Invest in relationships with those closest to you. Live freely and generously, in a spirit of open handedness. Life is best enjoyed alongside others. Share experiences, make memories, laugh often. There is deep joy to be found in living a communal life.

Being part of a group not only brings security and a sense of identity but let's face it, everything seems more enjoyable if we can have the chance to share it with someone else. Don't battle on alone but ask for help when you need it. Ask advice when you are in a dilemma about something. Skill swap. Share what you know or what you have been gifted with others.

Gratitude:

I have come to realise that every single moment is a precious gift. Don't get too wrapped up in your own internal dialogue to notice what's around you. Learn to look around and be attentive. What do you see? Notice the little things – a dew covered spider web, a colony of busy ants, the craftsmanship of a wrought iron gate.

There's wonder all around if we just take time to notice. Pay attention to what you can hear – the ticking clock, birdsong, music, your own heartbeat. Don't forget your other senses too – aromas, textures, tastes. There's a whole world waiting to be discovered. Be thankful. Appreciate everything.

***

I think back to those words spoken over me at the start of the journey....

"Stand at the crossroads and look; ask for the ancient paths, ask where the good way is and walk in it, and you will find rest for your souls." (Jeremiah 6:16 NIV)

I earnestly believe there is great truth to be gleaned from those words for all of us, regardless of religious belief, if we would only listen. They contain the secret of living a contented life. The words contain advice, written over two thousand years ago but are still so relevant today. In fact, they may be even more relevant today than at any other time in history. So, what advice do they hold? They advise us to take stock, reassess, change path and find the best way to live.

The first step is to decide to *'stand'* still enough for a moment to assess where we are in our lives. Taking time out and pausing to question ourselves is vitally important. Are you content with the direction your life is taking? Do you feel happy? Or are you stressed out? Too busy? Rushing through life? Pressing 'pause' is not easy for anyone in today's world, with all its pressures, expectations and hectic schedules. It requires a deliberate effort on our part to make time and create space for this to happen.

But happen it must if we are to find true freedom and a different, more balanced way of living. It may not be possible for you to take a nine week break away from your work and family commitments to walk from one end of the country to the other but we can all make time if necessary. Blocking specific periods of time into your schedule for 'development' can work just as well. Take yourself off to a quiet place, inside or out, armed with a notebook and pen and give yourself time to think. Turn off your phone. Think about what's important to you and start there.

Having carved out time to stop and ponder, we then need to *'look'* at the direction we are currently heading and the options available to us. Is there a different path we could take? Is there any possibility of a different way of doing life? In an ideal world, what would life look like for you? It's up to us, each one of us, to make a deliberate proactive choice, rather than simply getting swept along by events, the demands of others or societal pressures. We all have a choice. To simply 'go with the flow' is a choice in and of itself. If that way to live is your choice, then so be it. I hope it brings you true happiness.

But for me as for many others, this way of living is not enough to deeply satisfy. Ticking things off your 'To Do' list can bring temporary feelings of satisfaction but what about long term? You may have accomplished every task you set yourself but find yourself exhausted, burnt out, spent at the end of the day. Is that really how you want to live your life?

The verse tells us there is help along the way. We all need the wisdom of others, whether it be good friends, family members or those that have trodden the paths before us. To '*ask*' is not a sign of weakness, as society would have us believe, but a sign of strength. We are constantly pressured to be self-sufficient, relying solely on our own skills and abilities, rather than seeking help. But we were not born to live alone. We are all part of a community. If this journey taught me anything, it was that there is a kinship in humanity. People want to help others. There is absolutely no shame in seeking advice as to a better way of living rather than simply existing.

Take time to discover the '*ancient paths*'. To me, this speaks of the old, time-proven ways of living a fulfilled and satisfied life. Consider the possibility that maybe the answer doesn't lie in new technologies making our lives 'easier'. Getting the latest android or apple device, purchasing a new electric car, even investing in a robotic vacuum that cleans your house while you sleep may not bring us long term contentment. Some of the poorest people in the world are among the happiest. They have discovered what our predecessors knew - the truth that 'stuff' does not bring contentment. So, ask yourself, what makes them so content? What is the long-lost secret of finding deep joy and fulfilment in our lives?

Search out the *'good way'*. Live your best life rather than settling for a mediocre existence. Life is short and is meant to be enjoyed, not endured. What do you want to build into your life? What makes you happy? What gives you energy? What makes you feel truly alive? How do you want to spend your time?

 Learn to *'walk in it'*. This is just so important – knowledge needs to be applied in real life. It needs to impact our behaviours and our routines on a daily basis, or it counts for nothing. And the result of all this applied wisdom? Well, we are given the assurance that if we pay attention to this advice, if we do all of the above, we will find that true sense of peace, we will ultimately find *'rest'* for our *'souls'*.

Having paused for a while, assessed where we currently find ourselves and the direction we are heading, explored the choices and options available to us, and sought the advice and wisdom of others, we find ourselves at a *'crossroad'*. Which path will we take?

Choose wisely my friend.

Your life depends upon it.

About The Author

Debbie Cunningham

Debbie lives in Hampshire with her husband. This is her first book. She loves all things environmental and enjoys connecting people of all ages to the natural world when she's not out dog walking.

Printed in Great Britain
by Amazon

16235758R00100